concrete5
Beginner's Guide

Create and customize your own website with the concrete5
Beginner's Guide

Remo Laubacher

BIRMINGHAM - MUMBAI

concrete5
Beginner's Guide

First published: March 2011

Production Reference: 1140311

Published by Packt Publishing Ltd.
32 Lincoln Road
Olton
Birmingham, B27 6PA, UK.

ISBN 978-1-849514-28-6

www.packtpub.com

Cover Image by Asher Wishkerman (a.wishkerman@mpic.de)

Credits

Author
Remo Laubacher

Reviewers
Alex Hutchinson
Franz Maruna
Shawn K. Quinn

Acquisition Editor
Sarah Cullington

Development Editor
Roger D'souza

Technical Editors
Vanjeet D'souza
Azharuddin Sheikh

Indexers
Monica Ajmera Mehta
Tejal Daruwale

Editorial Team Leader
Akshara Aware

Project Team Leader
Priya Mukherji

Project Coordinator
Sneha Harkut

Proofreader
Aaron Nash

Graphics
Nilesh Mohite

Production Coordinator
Shantanu Zagade

Cover Work
Shantanu Zagade

About the Author

Remo Laubacher grew up in Central Switzerland in a small village surrounded by lots of mountains and natural beauty. He started working with computers when he was 10 years old and then, after various computer related projects, focused on ERP and Oracle development. After completing his BSc in Business Administration, Remo became a Partner at Ortic, his ERP and Oracle business. His interest and up-to-date knowledge of the latest web technologies allows him the freedom to work in website development. At mesch.ch—where he works as a website consultant—Remo discovered concrete5 as the perfect tool for their web related projects and has since become a key member of the c5 community. His tutorials can be found at `http://www.codeblog.ch`

To Ida, the best mother you can have.

About the Reviewers

Alex Hutchinson spent 15 years in the Telecommunications industry as a Technical Consultant for a Tier 1 carrier in London. In 2004, he set up MadeForSpace.com with his wife Jo, an editorial and production consultant. Website development was the result of their combination of publishing and technical skills and their passion for online access and communication. Alex discovered concrete5 at the end of 2009 and has been an avid fan and member of the community since then. Having enjoyed working on projects with Remo Laubacher in the past, Alex has been shown the light on the inner workings of this fantastic Content Management System.

He divides his time between London, where he meets with his clients, and Andalucía in Spain where he lives next to the beach with his wife Jo and young daughter Emily.

Shawn K. Quinn is a lifelong computer and technology enthusiast with gifted intellect. Shawn's love affair with technology began with an Atari 1200XL computer, which he taught himself how to program in both BASIC and 6502 assembly language. Prior to the prominence of the World Wide Web, Shawn was a BBS enthusiast, including some time as a sysop of his own bulletin board, originally running under TAG and later under Maximus. Today, he is an avid user of both concrete5 and WordPress for website development. Shawn heads an up-and-coming marketing and publicity consulting firm, Hamster Powered Creative, with a website at `http://www.hamsterpoweredcreative.com`, and also has a personal website at `http://www.shawnkquinn.com`. His interests outside of computing include poker, backgammon, chess, photography, the arts, camping, and Renaissance festivals.

I'd like to thank my friend Nick, who has stuck by me through almost two decades after many other friends have came and went; my friend Isabella, who helped me summon the courage to accept the opportunity to help edit this book when it was offered; and my friends Larry, Bill, Kelsey, Laban, Ed, Elaine, Ingrid, Ruth, and Trish (among others) for additional moral support; my mom, Carla Quinn, who helped nurture my desire to learn about computers from an early age, and who has never given up on me through the years; my grandmother, Gloria Quinn, who has rescued me from quite a few bad situations; and last but certainly not the least, I'd like to thank my grandfather, George Quinn (who left us in 2002), an absolutely spectacular grandfather to me while he was alive, who will be missed.

www.PacktPub.com

Support files, eBooks, discount offers and more

You might want to visit www.PacktPub.com for support files and downloads related to your book.

Did you know that Packt offers eBook versions of every book published, with PDF and ePub files available? You can upgrade to the eBook version at www.PacktPub.com and as a print book customer, you are entitled to a discount on the eBook copy. Get in touch with us at service@packtpub.com for more details.

At www.PacktPub.com, you can also read a collection of free technical articles, sign up for a range of free newsletters and receive exclusive discounts and offers on Packt books and eBooks.

http://PacktLib.PacktPub.com

Do you need instant solutions to your IT questions? PacktLib is Packt's online digital book library. Here, you can access, read and search across Packt's entire library of books.

Why Subscribe?

- Fully searchable across every book published by Packt
- Copy and paste, print and bookmark content
- On demand and accessible via web browser

Free Access for Packt account holders

If you have an account with Packt at www.PacktPub.com, you can use this to access PacktLib today and view nine entirely free books. Simply use your login credentials for immediate access.

Instant Updates on New Packt Books

Get notified! Find out when new books are published by following *@PacktEnterprise* on Twitter, or the *Packt Enterprise* Facebook page.

Table of Contents

Preface

The concrete5 Beginner's Guide will show you how to get up and running with concrete5 as quickly and painlessly as possible. Taking you from installation to deployment, this is the only reference that you will need for creating your new concrete5 site.

By using a number of real-world examples, as well as taking you through the set up of a sample site, this book will enable you to become familiar with all of concrete5's features. Use add-ons, themes, and blocks to give your site the look and feel that you desire. Simple PHP will enable you to customize the layout and navigation options of your site as well as extend the dashboard, giving you a fully functional, professional site in no time.

What this book covers

Chapter 1, Installation is all about the installation. You'll get a web server up and running on your local computer which you'll then use to install concrete5.

Chapter 2, Working with concrete5; before you start customizing the site a few words about using concrete5, the part which end users should know about concrete5.

Chapter 3, Permissions; concrete5 offers a lot of different permissions you can use to restrict certain actions on your site. You'll have a small protected section on your site once you're done with this chapter.

Chapter 4, Add-ons looks at add-ons: what types there are, where you can find them, and so on. This is the big picture before we start digging deeper.

Chapter 5, Creating Your Own Theme; every site has to have a personal touch, and this is where you'll learn how to create your own concrete5 theme to change the layout to the way you want it to be.

Chapter 6, Customizing Block Layout will show how concrete5 uses blocks as content elements. These elements can be styled as well as themes to get even more out of concrete5.

Chapter 7, Advanced Navigation; creating a navigation isn't complicated but there are a few things you have to know if you want to customize the navigation.

Chapter 8, Creating Your Own Add-on Block; while you can customize a lot by changing the layout, you might be in the situation where you need a completely new function in your site; check this chapter to get more information about that.

Chapter 9, Everything in a Package; being able to customize and extend almost everything can make things a bit messy. Have a look at this chapter to see how you can wrap things in a package for an easier handling.

Chapter 10, Dashboard Extension; block add-ons are great to manage the output of your site but sometimes there are things you have to do in the background. You'll have an extension which checks broken links in your site as well as a few smaller examples to manage your site.

Chapter 11, Deployment and Configuration; apart from a few configurations not needed on a daily basis, we're just moving the site and add-ons we've created so far to another server.

Who this book is for

This book is ideal for developer who would like to build their first site with concrete5. You will need to be a little bit familiar with PHP, MySQL and HTML but will likely have little to no experience in using concrete5.

Conventions

In this book, you will find several headings appearing frequently.

To give clear instructions of how to complete a procedure or task, we use:

Time for action – heading

1. Action 1
2. Action 2
3. Action 3

Instructions often need some extra explanation so that they make sense, so they are followed with:

What just happened?

This heading explains the working of tasks or instructions that you have just completed.

You will also find some other learning aids in the book, including:

Pop quiz – heading

These are short multiple choice questions intended to help you test your own understanding.

Have a go hero – heading

These set practical challenges and give you ideas for experimenting with what you have learned.

You will also find a number of styles of text that distinguish between different kinds of information. Here are some examples of these styles, and an explanation of their meaning.

Code words in text are shown as follows: "We can include other contexts through the use of the include directive."

A block of code is set as follows:

```php
<?php
for ($i = 0; $i < count($cArray); $i++ ) {
    $cobj = $cArray[$i];
    $title = $cobj->getCollectionName();
?>
```

When we wish to draw your attention to a particular part of a code block, the relevant lines or items are set in bold:

```php
<?php
for ($i = 0; $i < count($cArray); $i++ ) {
    $cobj = $cArray[$i];
    $title = $cobj->getCollectionName(); }
?>
```

New terms and **important words** are shown in bold. Words that you see on the screen, in menus or dialog boxes for example, appear in the text like this: "If you edit a page, you can click on **Design**".

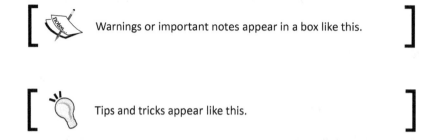

Warnings or important notes appear in a box like this.

Tips and tricks appear like this.

Reader feedback

Feedback from our readers is always welcome. Let us know what you think about this book—what you liked or may have disliked. Reader feedback is important for us to develop titles that you really get the most out of.

To send us general feedback, simply send an e-mail to feedback@packtpub.com, and mention the book title via the subject of your message.

If there is a book that you need and would like to see us publish, please send us a note in the **SUGGEST A TITLE** form on www.packtpub.com or e-mail suggest@packtpub.com.

If there is a topic that you have expertise in and you are interested in either writing or contributing to a book, see our author guide on www.packtpub.com/authors.

Customer support

Now that you are the proud owner of a Packt book, we have a number of things to help you to get the most from your purchase.

Errata

Although we have taken every care to ensure the accuracy of our content, mistakes do happen. If you find a mistake in one of our books—maybe a mistake in the text or the code—we would be grateful if you would report this to us. By doing so, you can save other readers from frustration and help us improve subsequent versions of this book. If you find any errata, please report them by visiting http://www.packtpub.com/support, selecting your book, clicking on the **errata submission form** link, and entering the details of your errata. Once your errata are verified, your submission will be accepted and the errata will be uploaded on our website, or added to any list of existing errata, under the Errata section of that title. Any existing errata can be viewed by selecting your title from http://www.packtpub.com/support.

Piracy

Piracy of copyright material on the Internet is an ongoing problem across all media. At Packt, we take the protection of our copyright and licenses very seriously. If you come across any illegal copies of our works, in any form, on the Internet, please provide us with the location address or website name immediately so that we can pursue a remedy.

Please contact us at copyright@packtpub.com with a link to the suspected pirated material.

We appreciate your help in protecting our authors, and our ability to bring you valuable content.

Questions

You can contact us at questions@packtpub.com if you are having a problem with any aspect of the book, and we will do our best to address it.

1
Installation

In this chapter you'll learn what you need to get your own concrete5 site up and running on your local computer. You don't need to have a lot of experience with Apache, PHP, and MySQL configuration as we're going to use XAMPP, which will install all the necessary components in almost no time.

Before you can start working with concrete5, you have to set up an environment where you can test and play around with concrete5 to get used to it. If you have a web hosting account, you can install concrete5 there, but since that isn't always the case, we'll install everything concrete5 needs to work smoothly on your local Windows computer.

The local webserver will only be used to build and test the site as well as the add-ons we're going to create. In the last chapter of this book, we're going to move the site from your local computer to a live webserver.

Preparing for installation

There are a few tools you'll need before you can start the installation process. You probably already work with similar tools, but let's still make sure you've got everything before continuing.

Web browser

concrete5 supports all major browsers as long as you're working with an up-to-date version. Please note: You can create a website which is viewable with Internet Explorer 6.0. The In-context editing system won't work with Internet Explorer 6.0 which means that you won't be able to update the content of your website, unless you use a more up-to-date web browser like Internet Explorer 7 or higher.

Whether you use Firefox, Chrome, Safari, or Internet Explorer doesn't really matter. concrete5 works with any recent browser with JavaScript capability, but it's recommended to use the latest browser version since most concrete5 community members test new releases with the newest browsers.

Text editor

Since we're going to edit lots of files you'll need a text editor. The requirements are quite small; you can pick almost any text editor you want. Just make sure it does support PHP syntax highlighting. If you don't work with PHP very often, here are some possible editors:

- **PSPad** (Windows only, free), `http://www.pspad.com`. A simple text editor with built-in FTP support. This can make a quick fix on your website even quicker.
- **Coda** (Mac OS only, commercial), `http://www.panic.com/coda/`. A very slick and clean editor, FTP support, CSS editor.
- **Notepad++** (Windows only, free), `http://notepad-plus-plus.org/`. A small and fast replacement for Windows notepad.

There are a lot more text editors, as mentioned previously; you can use almost any editor you want. If you're familiar with another product, just go with it. You won't find anything in this book where you need a special text editor feature.

Archive utility

The same with the file archive utility; there are plenty of tools you can use as long as it extracts standard ZIP files. If you don't have any archive utility installed, you can go with **IZArc** `http://www.izarc.org/`; it's free and does a good job.

FTP client

Once more, there are lots of choices. You'll have to change file permissions later, so make sure your FTP client includes this option. A powerful and well known client is **FileZilla**, `http://filezilla-project.org/`. It's free as well and has a lot more features than we need.

XAMPP installation

If you think you've found all the tools you'd like to use to create your website, you're ready to install XAMPP.

Time for action – installing XAMPP

concrete5 is a PHP application which uses PHP as its programming language in combination with a MySQL database. There are lots of possibilities to meet the requirements of concrete5. The preferred web server is Apache, IIS should work as well but isn't supported by the core team, even if it isn't as well tested as Apache.

If you already have a server or a local Apache, PHP, and MySQL setup, you can skip this step and continue with downloading concrete5. Otherwise, you are going to need to install XAMPP on your local computer by following these simple steps:

1. Go to `http://www.apachefriends.org/` and click on **XAMPP for Windows**. Scroll down and download the latest version of XAMPP Lite. If you're not very familiar with these tools, you should download the EXE and not the ZIP. Double-click the EXE as soon as it has been downloaded. You should see the following window:

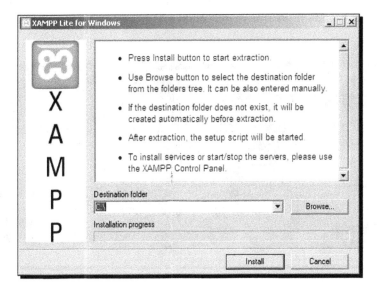

2. Click **Install** to start the installation process; it will take a while as it extracts quite a lot of files. You can install XAMPP in your program directory `C:\Program Files` but it won't work on Vista unless you modify some privileges. If you don't feel comfortable changing your security settings, just use `C:\` instead.

If you want to know more about the security changes needed on Vista to install XAMPP in your program directory, go to this page and follow the instructions: `http://www.apachefriends.org/en/faq-xampp-windows.html#vista`

3. After the installation has completed you'll see an old fashioned console window asking a few questions. They look like this; you can confirm all default values:

4. At the end you'll see a menu where you can execute different actions. You'll later have to start the **XAMPP Control Panel** but let's leave this screen untouched for now; we have to make one modification first.

Before you start XAMPP, you should change one MySQL setting. MySQL table names are not case sensitive on Windows. This will cause some problems if you want to move your site to a Linux server where MySQL is by default set up with case sensitive table names. It's therefore recommended to change this, if you work with concrete5:

5. Go to the directory where you've installed XAMPP, open `mysql` and then `bin`. It should look like the following:

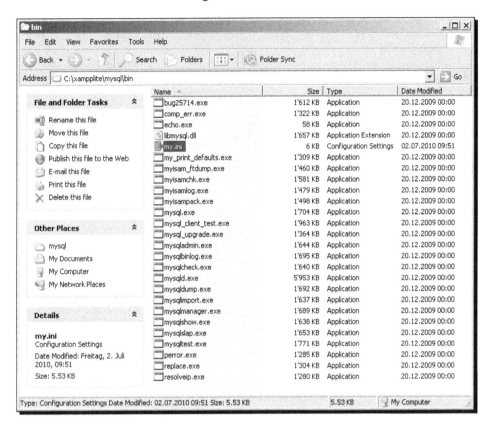

6. The `my.ini` file contains several settings related to MySQL. Open the file and locate the section `mysqld` and insert the following line:

```
lower_case_table_names = 0
```

The first lines should then look like the following:

```
# Example MySQL config file for medium systems.
#
# This is for a system with little memory (32M - 64M)
# where MySQL plays an important part, or systems
# up to 128M where MySQL is used together with
# other programs (such as a web server)
#
# You can copy this file to
# /etc/my.cnf to set global options,
# mysql-data-dir/my.cnf to set server-specific options
```

```
# (in this installation this directory is @localstatedir@)
# or
# ~/.my.cnf to set user-specific options.
#
# In this file, you can use all long options that a
# program supports.
# If you want to know which options a program supports,
# run the program with the "--help" option.

# The following options will be passed to all MySQL clients
[client]
#user           = your_username
#password       = your_password
host            = .
port            = 3306
socket          = "MySQL"


# Here follows entries for some specific programs

# The MySQL server
[mysqld]
lower_case_table_names   = 0
basedir                  = "C:/xampplite/mysql/"
datadir                  = "C:/xampplite/mysql/data/"
port            = 3306
socket          = "MySQL"
skip-locking
key_buffer               = 16M
max_allowed_packet       = 1M
table_cache              = 64
sort_buffer_size         = 512K
net_buffer_length        = 8K
read_buffer_size         = 256K
read_rnd_buffer_size     = 512K
myisam_sort_buffer_size  = 8M
```

Downloading the example code for this book

You can download the example code files for all Packt books you have purchased from your account at http://www.PacktPub.com. If you purchased this book elsewhere, you can visit http://www.PacktPub.com/support and register to have the files e-mailed directly to you.

7. Now that MySQL is properly configured, go back to the XAMPP console menu and enter 1 to open the control panel where you can start and stop all components. You should see the following window:

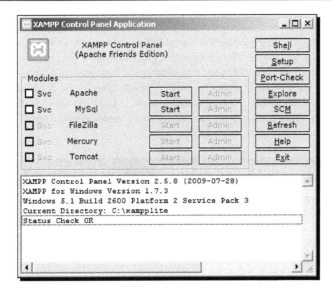

8. Start both Apache and MySQL, and your web server will be up and running in no time, ready for concrete5!

9. If everything worked you should be able to open your browser and enter `http://localhost/`. On this screen you can select your preferred language and you'll see a nice status page about XAMPP.

> It might just happen that Apache doesn't start because port 80 is already used by an application like Skype. You can click on **Port-Check** to see if there are any ports being used before you start the XAMPP services. If there are, either disable the other services, or reconfigure, or stop them.

What just happened?

The XAMPP setup package installed a working web server, including PHP with the most commonly used modules and a MySQL database. This is what a lot of web applications need, an environment which works for a lot of web applications and CMS's as well.

You've also had a quick look at one MySQL configuration file to avoid problems when moving your data to a Linux server. If you want to know more about this setting, the MySQL documentation is going to answer almost any question about table names: `http://dev.mysql.com/doc/refman/5.1/en/identifier-case-sensitivity.html`.

Please don't forget, XAMPP is by default a user-friendly and simple system but insecure to simplify the development process as much as possible. It is nice to work with and great for your first experience with your own web server, but not recommended for a production environment. Later in this book, we'll move your site to a LAMP server (Linux, Apache, MySQL, and PHP) which is more widely used by webhosting companies with a more secure configuration.

Pop quiz – requirements for concrete5

Like any other software, concrete5 needs certain things to run. Try to answer which of the following items are true:

1. Which of the following server-side programming language(s) has been used to build concrete5?

    a. PHP

    b. Microsoft ASP

    c. Java

    d. All of the above

2. Which of the following database(s) can you use with concrete5?

    a. PostgreSQL

    b. MySQL

    c. Oracle

    d. All of the above

3. Which of the following operating system(s) can you use to run concrete5?

    a. Microsoft Windows

    b. Mac OS X

    c. Linux

    d. All of the above

4. Name the webserver(s) you can use to run concrete5.

    a. Microsoft IIS

    b. Nginx

    c. Apache

    d. lighttpd

Downloading concrete5

Your local web server is running, there is nothing else to prepare, and you are ready to install concrete5 now. There are just a few more steps till you can log in to concrete5.

Time for action – downloading the latest version

Before we can install anything we have to get the latest concrete5 version from this URL: `http://www.concrete5.org/developers/downloads/` and follow these steps:

1. Open the ZIP archive and extract all the files to `C:\xampplite\htdocs`. Override the files which are already in the directory.

2. After you've extracted the ZIP file you should see a structure like the following:

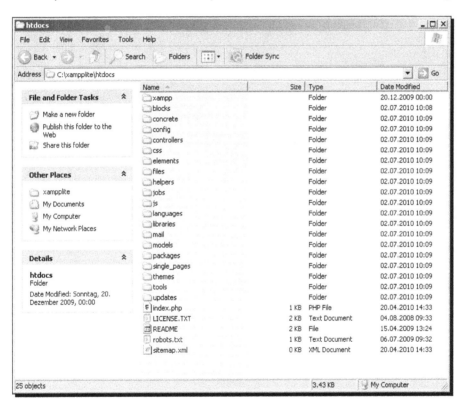

 At the time of writing, concrete5 v5.4.1.1 was the latest version. You can download a newer version if available; changes in the installation process should be minor if there are any at all.

What just happened?

You've downloaded and extracted the concrete5 CMS files. Depending on your archive utility it might have been the case that empty folders like `updates`, `files`, and others hadn't been created. Make sure your structure looks like the one shown in the preceding screenshot.

Before we continue, a few words about the file structure you've just created. It's important that you understand the structure of concrete5 before you start working with it. It's helpful to have a clear understanding about the structure so you can find your files easily. You'll later see that all add-ons in the marketplace follow this structure. Using the suggested structure helps to keep a clean structure, no matter who builds the concrete5 site or add-on.

It might look a bit bulky to have so many folders in the root of your website but you'll realize that it makes perfect sense to have this structure the more you work with concrete5. To give you a first impression about the most important folders:

Folder	Explanation
blocks	Put your custom blocks in this folder; you'll learn more about blocks in the next few chapters.
concrete	Probably the most important part; this is where all core files, the actual CMS, is located. Never update anything in this folder.
config	The folder where concrete5 puts the configuration files.
files	The file manager stores your files in this directory.
packages	This is where you have to put add-ons if you install them manually.
updates	The concrete5 auto update feature puts the new core in this directory.

There are a few more folders but you probably won't need them unless you dive deep into concrete5. We won't use them in this book and therefore won't mention them.

Creating an empty SQL database

You must create an empty SQL database before you can install concrete5.

Time for action – creating an empty SQL database

Use phpMyAdmin which is included in XAMPP Lite to create the database:

1. Open `http://localhost/phpmyadmin/` or hit the **Admin** button next to **MySQL** in the XAMPP control panel and you should see the following page:

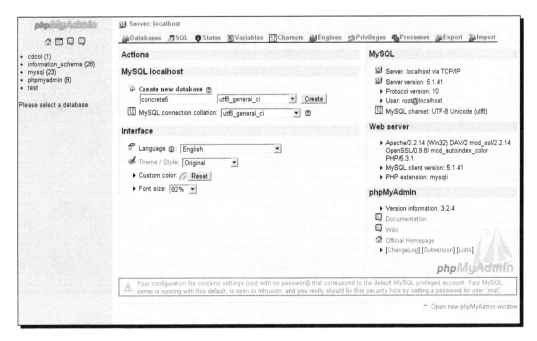

2. Enter **concrete5** as the database name.

3. Select the collation **utf8_general_ci**.

4. Hit **Create**.

5. Go to the **Privileges** tab and click on **Add a new User** to create a dedicated user for concrete5.

6. When prompted, use the following credentials to fill in the following fields:

- ❏ User Name: `concrete5`

- ❏ Host: `localhost`
  This makes sure that the user can only be used if the database is accessed by the local machine.

- ❏ Password: `concrete5`
  The password to access your database. Feel free to use a more secure password than concrete5, just make sure you remember it when we Install concrete5 in the next step.

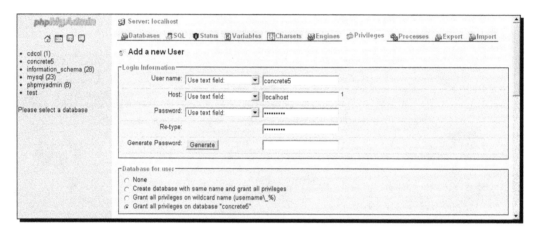

7. Hit **Go** and the user is available and your database is ready for concrete5!

What just happened?

All the components are ready; Apache including PHP should be running and there's an empty MySQL database to host your concrete5 site.

 Please note: concrete5 can't be installed in a database which isn't empty!

Installing concrete5

We're finally ready to get to the concrete5 part. Let's install it!

Time for action – installing concrete5

To install concrete5, follow these steps:

1. Open your favorite browser and enter `http://localhost/`. You should see the installation screen:

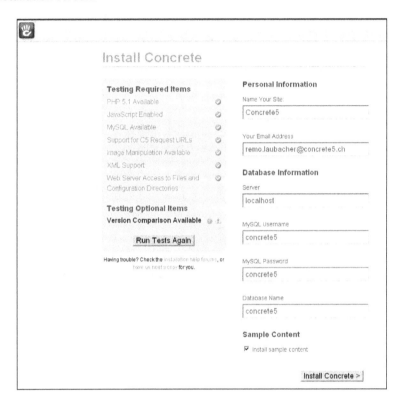

2. On the left there are a few checks to make sure that your web server meets all the requirements of concrete5. A few words about the required items:

- ❏ **PHP**: Whenever possible, try to use the latest PHP version.

- ❏ **JavaScript and MySQL**: At this point, concrete5 only works with MySQL and needs JavaScript because of its AJAX interface.

- ❏ **C5 Request URLs**: By default you'll see `index.php` in each concrete5 URL you open. To get rid of this, you need to have the Apache module `mod_rewrite`, which we're going to deal with later in this chapter.

- ❏ **Image Manipulation and XML Support**: These are PHP modules which are enabled by default and needed by concrete5.

❏ **Web Server Access to Files**: Usually not a problem if you work with XAMPP on Windows. The webserver must be able to write some files in your website's installation directory. We'll discuss this issue later, when we move the site to the production server.

❏ **Version Comparison**: This feature uses Python to show you the difference between page modifications. A nice feature but it doesn't work because XAMPP Lite doesn't install Python. But since it's optional we're not going to worry about it.

3. To install concrete5 you have to enter the following personal information:

❏ **Name Your Site**: Any name you want—can be changed in the dashboard later.

❏ **Your Email Address**: The admin mail address. Make sure it exists; this is where you'll receive a link to change the eventually forgotten admin password.

4. You will also have to enter the following database information:

❏ **Server**: Since the database is running on the same machine as the web server, just enter `localhost`.

❏ **MySQL Username**, **MySQL Password**, and **Database Name**: concrete5 or whatever you used when you created the user in phpMyAdmin.

5. **Sample Content**: If you enable this, concrete5 will create a few sample pages to play around with. Enable this, if you're new to concrete5, it will create some nice pages where you can see the different blocks you can use to build your website.

6. If you've entered all the necessary information, click **Install Concrete >**!

What just happened?

A few seconds after you've clicked **Install Concrete** you should see a screen with an automatically generated admin password. Make sure you don't lose it.

concrete5 is installed and ready to work with on your computer!

You should now be able to open the default concrete5 website, by entering `http://localhost/` in your browser.

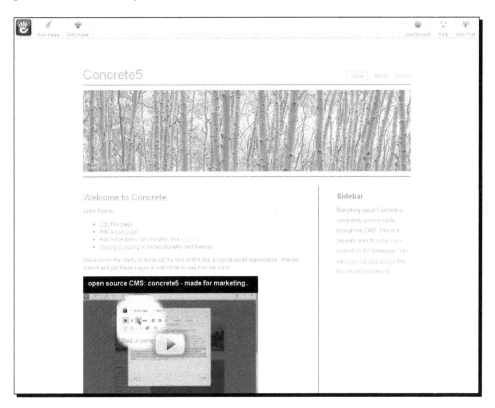

The configuration file

After you've successfully installed concrete5 you'll find a file called `site.php` in the `config` directory. This is where the installation process has saved the information you've entered during the process. Here's how it looks:

```php
<?php
define('DB_SERVER', 'localhost');
define('DB_USERNAME', 'concrete5');
define('DB_PASSWORD', 'password');
define('DB_DATABASE', 'concrete5');
define('BASE_URL', 'http://localhost');
define('DIR_REL', '');
define('PASSWORD_SALT',
'zc8tSsYQI0E2MifRwboxBq6K9UmbL4X7vrf3Tz1unNFVCPWkO5glHjZaGpADJ');
?>
```

- ◆ DB_SERVER, DB_USERNAME, DB_PASSWORD, and DB_DATABASE are obviously just database related. If the credentials to access your MySQL database have changed, this is where you have to modify them to make sure concrete5 can access your database.

- ◆ BASE_URL is used by default to make sure that your website visitors use your primary domain. If your site is accessible by multiple domains, concrete5 will just forward them to the URL specified in BASE_URL.

- ◆ DIR_REL is empty if you've installed your website in the root. It's only filled if your website is located in a subdirectory.

- ◆ PASSWORD_SALT, this is a random string and is used in combination with the password to generate the password hashes found in the user table. Salts are used to complicate dictionary attacks and even if they are useless without a password you should still not publish a real password salt to keep your site safe.

Pop quiz – the configuration file

1. You'll often have to check or modify a few lines in the configuration file, so where can you find it?

    a. `<concrete5 installation directory>\config.php`

    b. `<concrete5 installation directory>\config\config.php`

    c. `<concrete5 installation directory>\config\site.php`

Pretty URLs

When you browse to a subpage in your concrete5 site you'll notice an odd thing in every URL: there's `index.php` in it like this `http://localhost/index.php/about/`. Every request to a page in concrete5 is processed by `index.php`. This has several advantages: It's easier to check the permissions, there's a single point where the page rendering time can be improved, and a few more things.

However, even with these advantages you probably wouldn't like to see `index.php` in every URL. Luckily it's rather easy to change it if your web server supports rewrite rules. XAMPP does, and here's what we have to do.

Time for action – enabling pretty URLs

Follow these steps to get rid of the `index.php` from you URLs:

1. Log in to concrete5.

2. Click on the **Dashboard** button in the top-right corner.

3. Select **Sitewide Settings** in the navigation.

4. Check **Enable Pretty URLs** and hit **Save**, you should see the following screen:

5. concrete5 should have created a file called `.htaccess` in the root of your website. This is the file where the rewrite rules are stored which remove `index.php` from the URLs.

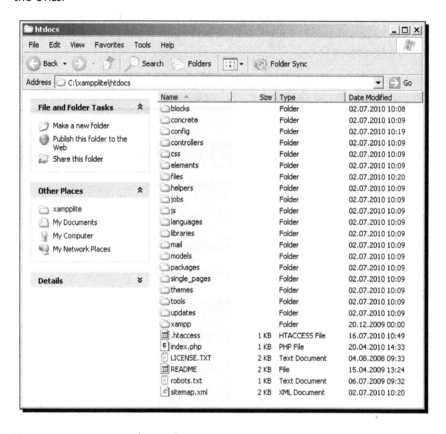

You can now open a subpage by entering `http://localhost/about/`—the `index.php` is gone.

What just happened?

Congratulations, you're done! concrete5 is running and you've also activated some options to improve the behavior of concrete5.

You've enabled pretty URLs which uses the Apache `mod_rewrite` module to rewrite URLs. In case you'd like to know more about this Apache feature this is the official documentation:

```
http://httpd.apache.org/docs/2.2/mod/mod_rewrite.html
```

.htaccess is a configuration file most commonly used by Apache to configure Apache modules on a directory level. It's a simple text file you can open with any text editor of your choice. If you haven't worked with Apache before, the content might be a bit confusing but concrete5 took care of it. You shouldn't have to modify anything on your own in this file.

 Pretty URLs can also be used with Microsoft IIS but you need to install a rewrite filter first.

If you want to try it on your own, you can find a solid and free rewrite filter at this address: http://iirf.codeplex.com/.

Summary

You've reached the end of Chapter 1!

- You should now have a working concrete5 installation from where you'll learn how to work with concrete5.
- In case you have to check or modify your concrete5 configuration, you should know where to find the files.
- We've looked at the requirements to run concrete5.
- All the tools you'll need to go though this book should be installed in your computer.
- We're going to use this test site to build our own site including some customization and programming.

2
Working with concrete5

In this chapter you'll learn how to use concrete5 to manage the content of your site. If you build websites for customers, this is the part your customers have to learn and understand. More precisely, you'll learn to add, edit, and remove content and you'll also learn how to insert columns and various text styles.

Getting familiar with concrete5

Before you start customizing and extending concrete5 you have to get familiar with the tools you'll need when you want to update your site's content. Since you don't want to let everyone update your site, you have to log in using the account which has been created during the installation. Let's go through this step by step:

Time for action – logging in to concrete5

Follow these steps to log in to concrete5:

1. If you followed the first chapter step by step you can enter `http://localhost/` and get to the default concrete5 home page.

2. At the bottom of the page you'll find a link **Sign In to Edit this Site**; click on it.

3. You can now log in with the user `admin` and the password generated during the installation process.

What just happened?

When you're logged in, you'll see the exact same page with one major difference. There's a toolbar on the top to execute certain actions on the current page.

The following table explains the different elements of the toolbar:

Button	Explanation
Edit Page	Before you can edit the content, you have to activate the edit mode, more details in the next Time for action section.
Add Page	This button adds a new page underneath the current page.
Dashboard	This brings up the administration panel where you can create users, Install add-ons, and a lot more.
Help	This buttons shows a small dialog with a link to the documentation, forums, and a search box to find existing posts in the concrete5 community.
Sign Out	Hit this button to log out of concrete5.

Adding new blocks

Now that we are in the in-site editing mode, we can start editing our site. This works by adding blocks to predefined areas. You'll see the different elements and standard blocks of concrete5 as we go through the next Time for action section step by step.

Time for action – adding new blocks

To add a new block to your concrete5 page follow these steps:

1. First, we would like to change some of the content on the home page. Click **Edit Page** to activate the edit mode on the page.

2. The look of the page changes a bit when you're in the edit mode but you're still able to see the actual page.

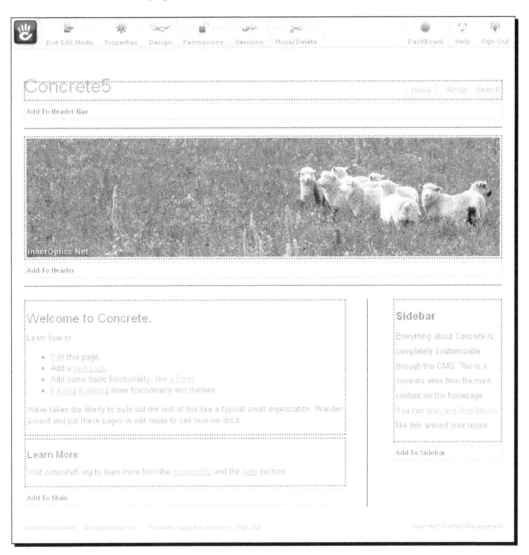

The default page type has four sections called **areas**. An area is a place where you can insert content. Unlike other CMS's, editable areas in concrete5 themes aren't specific to a content type.

What does this mean? If you create a theme you just specify where the user can place content. You don't add any restriction to the content type by default.

The content elements are called **blocks** and can be put in any area several times. This offers great flexibility; you can put a slideshow, a form, and a lot more stuff anywhere you want.

3. At the bottom of each area you can find a link called **Add To <Area-Name>**. It displays a small menu with different actions, as shown:

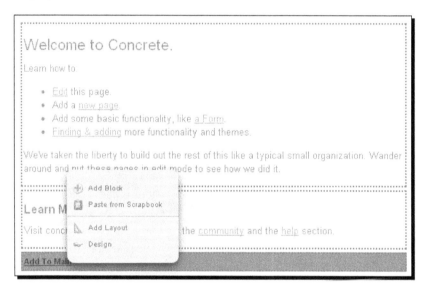

4. Right now, we only need **Add Block**. We're going to use the other items later in this chapter. If you click on it, you'll see a dialog with all available blocks. By default concrete5 ships with the following blocks:

❑ **Content**: Insert formatted text using a WYSIWYG editor.

❑ **HTML**: For those who know HTML, this lets you insert plain HTML code.

❑ **Auto-Nav**: Necessary to build a dynamic navigation. We'll cover this block at full length later in this book.

❑ **External Form**: Lets you build a form using an MVC approach. Programming experience highly recommended.

❑ **Form**: Offers a nice and easy to way to build forms. Not as flexible as an external form but it doesn't require any HTML or PHP coding!

❑ **Page List**: Displays a set of pages. It can be used to build a simple news list or blog.

❑ **File**: Insert a download link to a file you've uploaded to the file manager.

❑ **Image**: Places content including a hover effect in the page.

❑ **Flash Content**: Use this block to insert a flash banner or animation.

❑ **Guestbook**: If you want your visitors to leave comments on your page, use this block.

❑ **Slideshow**: Creates an image slideshow with a smooth transition in just a few clicks.

❑ **Search**: Displays a form to let the visitors search for pages on your website.

❑ **Google Map**: Uses a Google map to show your visitors where they can find your company.

❑ **Video Player**: Plays videos in different formats.

❑ **RSS Displayer**: Pulls news articles from another page by including an RSS news feed.

❑ **Youtube Video**: Puts your Youtube video on your website.

❑ **Survey**: Creates a simple survey and displays the result using a pie chart.

5. Let's start by selecting **Content** to insert a new formatted text block. Another dialog will pop up and display a WYSIWYG editor where you can enter text, including images and links to other pages. It mostly works like any other text editing application. You've got text formatting, some paragraph formats that you'll probably know if you've been working with Internet technology before.

6. It should be pretty intuitive, but please have a quick look at the toolbar on the top of the text area. If you want to insert a link to a concrete5 page or a file from the file manager you have to use the toolbar above the text area.

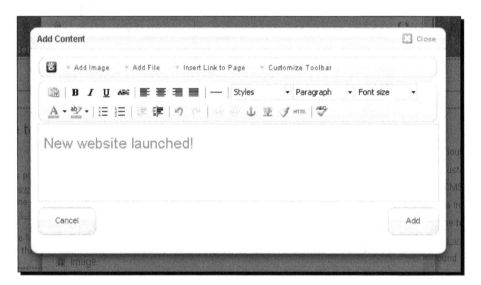

7. Click **Add** and your text is part of the page!

What just happened?

You should understand how concrete5 changes the way a page looks when you enter the edit mode. This is also one feature that makes concrete5 different from other CMS'; you can edit the content in a view which looks a lot like the actual page.

We did have a quick look at the way concrete5 places content on your pages. You should also have a first impression about the default blocks you can use when you install the standard concrete5 distribution.

Your playground site should also contain some words you've entered using the content block.

Now that you've added a new block, you should also try to edit an existing block.

Time for action – editing existing blocks

Follow these steps to edit an existing block on your site:

1. Once a block has been added, you can simply edit it again by clicking on it. The following menu appears with different options:

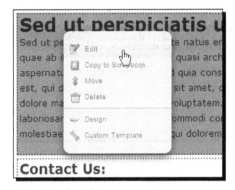

- ❑ **Edit**: this shows you the block editing block you've seen when you added a new instance of the block.

- ❑ **Copy to Scrapbook**: this copies the block into the scrapbook from where you can use it at different places. Don't worry about it at the moment, as there's a section about the scrapbook later in this chapter.

- ❑ **Move**: click on this element to switch into a different mode where you can drag blocks around to reorder them.

- ❑ **Delete**: you don't need the block anymore? Hit this button and it's removed from the page.

- ❑ **Design**: this lets you style the blocks by using some CSS rules. There's another *Time for action* section about this later in this chapter.

- ❑ **Custom Template**: some blocks ship with different templates to change the look of the output. We're going to have a detailed look at this feature in *Chapter 6*.

What just happened?

We had a quick look at editing an existing block. There's not much; once you know how to add a block, editing it is usually pretty much the same. You click on the block, select **Edit**, and update the values you've previously entered.

Have a go hero – adding more blocks

As you've seen in the previous chapter, concrete5 ships with a lot more blocks than just the content block we've discussed. Try to add and edit all the blocks you can use to get familiar with concrete5. It's going to be routine when updating page content!

Time for action – exiting edit mode

Once you're done editing the page, you have several options in the toolbar which changed when you entered the in-site editing mode.

1. The obvious first choice is **Exit Edit Mode**. It's what you'll need when you're done editing the site. However, when you've added new content, there are several choices you'll see when you hit that button:

    □   **Discard My Edits**: Exit the edit mode and drop all changes.

    □   **Preview My Edits**: This will create a new page version, but won't approve it, hence keeping it hidden from the public.

    □   **Publish My Edits**: Save changes and publish them, making all changes visible to the public immedlately. Click on this button in our case.

2. **Properties**, **Design**, **Permissions**, and **Versions** are accessible from your site's dashboard as well. We'll cover them in the dashboard section of this chapter.

3. **Move/Delete** will show you a dialog where you can either select the new parent page for the current page or delete it, if you don't need it anymore.

Pop quiz – concrete5 in-site editing mode

Try to remember the things you can do while you're in the in-site editing mode.

1. What kind of blocks can you add to a concrete5 page?

2. What buttons can you see in the toolbar while you're editing a page?

3. What buttons are available once you leave the edit mode?

The dashboard

Even with the really slick in-site editing system, there are still some tasks you can't do while you're browsing the site. This is why there's still a dashboard where you can find several options and forms to modify your concrete5 site.

While you're browsing the site while logged in, there's always a button called **Dashboard** in the top right corner. Click on it and you should get to the dashboard.

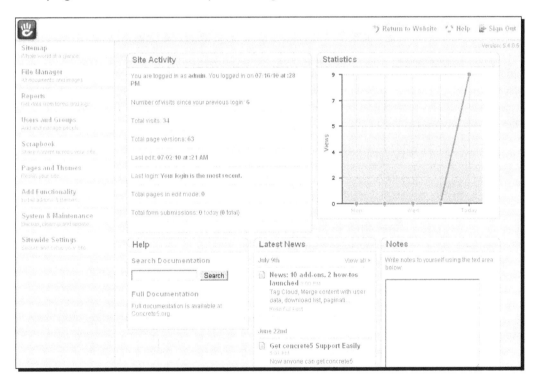

We'll quickly go through all the items but won't cover all the details as it would take too much time. Most parts on the dashboard are easy to understand anyway—take some time and patience and you'll probably be able to figure out most of the options on the dashboard very quickly. At the end of this section is a list with all the items we haven't mentioned; just follow the next paragraphs and take some time at the end to play around with the rest.

When you open the dashboard you'll see the following boxes:

Item	Explanation
Site Activity	Some hints about the site activity, the current users, some statistical numbers, and a note about form submissions.
Statistics	concrete5 contains simple site statistics which show you the number of page views right in the dashboard.
Help	This search box crawls through the concrete5.org documentation and community posts.
Latest News	These items are directly pulled from concrete5.org, news about releases, new items published in the community – everything you need to know about concrete5.
Notes	In case you tend to forget things. A small text area to write notes to yourself.

On the left you can find a few navigation items. This should only give you a rough overview; we will cover the most important things later in this book. Just try to remember the things you can find in the dashboard, it will make it easier to find the tools you need once you're more used to working with concrete5.

Item	Explanation
Sitemap	While you can edit the page content easily using the in-site editing system, it can still be very helpful to see a hierarchical page structure of your website.
File Manager	When files are used in concrete5 they are uploaded using the file manager. These are the things you can do here: ◆ Upload and delete files ◆ Manage files using sets ◆ Assign attributes to files
Reports	Some blocks like the survey or form block report data which you can find under this section any time you want. There's also an option to export the data to Excel.
Users and Groups	An essential part to manage your permissions. We're going through this step by step in the next chapter. Here, you are able to: ◆ Manage users ◆ Create and assign groups to users ◆ Attach attributes to users

Item	Explanation
Scrapbook	If you want to replicate a block across a site, add it to the scrapbook. There's an example later in this chapter.
Pages and Themes	This allows you to: ♦ Install and activate themes ♦ Create and edit page types ♦ Add new page attributes ♦ Create single pages
Add Functionality	This allows you to install and update concrete5 add-ons.
System & Maintenance	Maintain your website by executing these tasks: ♦ Back up and restore your database in case you want to try something and need the ability to go back to a previous state. ♦ Update to a newer version of concrete5 if available. ♦ Run jobs to index your site for the search functionality, creation of a `sitemap.xml` for Google and process e-mails if you're using the concrete5 community feature.
Sitewide Settings	Lots of settings, change the rich-text editor toolbar, restrict access to your site, some developer related information and more. We're going to look at a few settings in the next chapter.

Pop quiz – dashboard features

Try to list the things you can find on the dashboard.

Adding more pages

concrete5 uses a sitemap to build a hierarchical tree of pages. This means that every page has one root page. The top level is **home** and can't be removed.

If you already have a web site project going on, you've probably thought about the hierarchical site structure for a bit. Use that structure if you have one, otherwise we're just going to add some random pages.

Time for action – adding pages to create a news section

Follow these steps to add new pages to your site:

1. When you're in the **Dashboard**, click on **Sitemap** to get to the following screen:

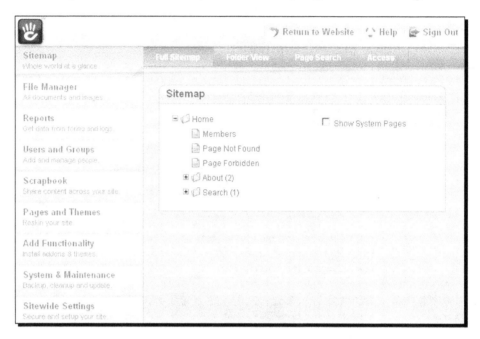

2. Click on the **Home** page and you'll be presented with a menu. Right now, we only need **Add Page**.

3. Click on **Add Page** to bring the dialog up where you can enter the information about the new page you want to create.

4. These are the field types as seen in the preceding screenshot. Enter the following information into each field:

    ❑ **Choose a Page Type**: When you're creating a theme you can add several page types to offer the end user different layouts like single-column, multi-column, and so on. We just select **Full Width** for now.

    ❑ **Name**: The name/title of your page. As we're going to create a new section, enter News.

    ❑ **Alias**: This is generated by concrete5 when you enter the name. You could change it if you want your page to be accessible using a different URL, but leave it how it is for now.

5. Click the **Add** button and you should see the updated sitemap.

6. The page we just created is going to hold all the news entries together. Let's add one sample entry by clicking on **News** to bring up the menu and selecting **Add Page** again. Select a page type of your choice and enter a page name. You should have another page underneath news:

What just happened?

After the new pages have been added, you can click on one and select **View** to see the page. There are already a few blocks in the new page, even if you didn't add any of them. concrete5 took all the blocks which are predefined in the defaults and added them to your new page.

You've also seen that there are different page types, each of which will result in a different page layout. Don't worry if you picked the wrong one; you can always hit the **Design** button in the toolbar, while you're in edit mode, to bring up the dialog where you can change the page type at any time.

We're going to add some more blocks to our page in the next time for action. After that we're going to look at page defaults to help you to understand how some of the blocks automatically appeared in the new page.

When you're logged in you can always hit **Add Page** in the toolbar on the top. This creates a child page to the current page. This can be done using the sitemap as well; it's just another way to add a new page.

Time for action – adding blocks to new page

Add new blocks to your page by following these steps:

1. Open the **News** page, it already works but we can't see our news entry. Makes sense; how should concrete5 know that we want to have a news list on this page? It can't, so let's help concrete5 and create that list manually.

2. Go into the edit mode by clicking on **Edit Page**.

3. Display the block list by clicking on **Add To Main**.

4. Select **Page List**.

5. Change the option in the middle **Location in Website** to **beneath this page**. This makes sure that only pages underneath news will be displayed. All other options can be left the way they are.

6. Click on **Add** to insert the list into your page.

7. Leave the edit mode by clicking on **Exit Edit Mode**.

8. Select **Publish My Edits** to confirm your changes.

9. Done!

What just happened?

There's a rather simple, but working, news section in your site which we'll improve later by adding some more advanced features.

Even if the website you're creating still looks boring, at least you've got a structure. This makes the design process easier as well, since you can easily add some content to your design and see how it looks in the website.

Have a go hero – adding more pages

You've seen how pages can be added to represent a news section. The sitemap should give you a good overview of your site. Try to add all the pages you think you need on your site, whatever you do in the sitemap it's not going to break anything.

◆ If you misspelled a page name, click on it and select **Properties.** You can change the name at any time.

◆ Selected the wrong page type? No problem, click on a page and hit **Design** and you'll see a dialog where you can select another page type.

Page defaults

There are situations where you might want to put the same block on several pages. For example: If your page has a picture in the head of each page, it would be helpful if there's a default picture block in each page you create. For a small page, the navigation is probably identical on each page.

In concrete5 you can manage not only the page content, but also the page type content. What does this mean? Since every page is derived from a page type, they behave like templates. Blocks in the page types are, by default, placed in every new page. It's also possible to add blocks to existing pages by modifying the page type defaults on each page as well.

Time for action – adding default blocks to a page type

Follow these steps to add default blocks to a page type:

1. Go to the dashboard and select **Pages and Themes**.

2. Click on the tab called **Page Types**.

3. On top of the screen, you can see a list with all available page types. Pick the one where you'd like to add some default blocks by clicking on **Defaults** in the row of the page type of your choice.

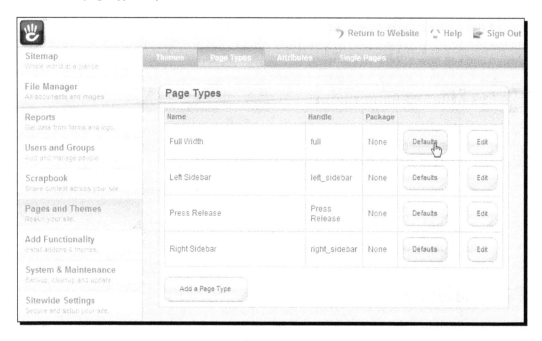

4. You'll be redirected to a screen which looks like a normal page but it's actually a page type you're going to edit. Start the edit mode by clicking on **Edit Page** in the top toolbar.

5. Click on **Add To Header** and select the image block, pick a file from the file manager, and hit **Add**.

6. Save the changes by clicking on **Exit Edit Mode** and confirm it by clicking on **Publish My Edits**.

What just happened?

By adding a block to the page type defaults, you've created a template-like page which will be copied to each page you're going to create from the same page type. Even if you're using this block in only 90% of all cases, you can still benefit from this feature. Removing or modifying a block which has been added by using the page defaults is no problem.

Adding blocks to existing sites

What if you added a block to a page type which you already used several times? For those pages where you didn't add the block, you can use a menu item only available when editing the page type defaults.

Click on the block you want to copy to the existing pages. Select **Setup on Child Pages** and mark the pages in the dialog where you want to copy the block. Confirm your selection by clicking on **Update** and all pages you've selected receive a copy of the block.

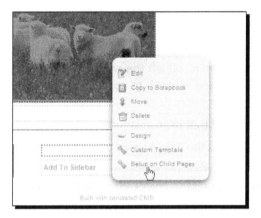

Page commands

When you click on a page in the sitemap, you can see several menu items to change anything about a page. **Properties**, **Set Permissions**, **Design**, **Versions**, **Delete**, and **Add Page** are also visible in the toolbar of the in-site editing mode. You'll see the same dialog, no matter where you've opened it. Please note: **Add Page** will only be visible when you're looking at a page without editing it, while the rest will be available when you actually edit a page.

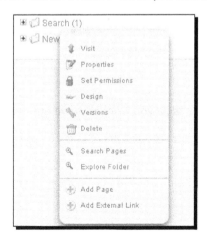

The following are the items present in the menu:

- **Visit:** Opens the selected page.

- **Properties:** Shows a dialog where you can edit the values you enter when you create a new page. Change page title and description, manage custom properties, and set aliases for a page if you want the page to appear at different URLs.

- **Set Permissions:** Manages the access to the page. More about this in the next chapter.

- **Design:** Changes the template or theme for the page.

- **Versions:** You want to see how the page looked in the past? Versions shows you every page version since it has been created. If you didn't publish a page change and only hit preview when you left the edit mode, you'll see a new unapproved page version in this dialog. Use this to approve the new version or go backwards and approve an older version.

- **Delete:** You don't need that page anymore? Delete it!

- **Search Pages:** Activates the **Page Search** tab and sets the current page as the parent page in the search dialog.

- **Explore Folders:** Brings up the **Folder View** for the current page.

- **Add Page:** We've used this item before, lets you add new pages.

- **Add External Link:** You can use this option if you don't need a page but just a link to another page which appears in your pages navigation.

Moving and sorting pages

While you are probably able to create a page structure without making a mistake, I'm not. Luckily it's very easy to move pages around.

Time for action – moving and sorting your pages

Follow these steps to restructure your pages:

1. Go to the **Sitemap**.

2. Click on the icon of the page you want to move but don't release the mouse button.

3. You can now drag the item around and change its position by dropping it between two other sitemap items.

4. If you drop the item on top of another page, the following dialog shows up:

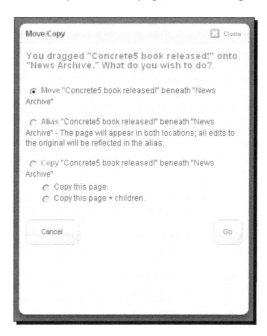

5. Instead of just being able to resort to your page, this dialog allows you to create an alias—a second URL for your page—as well as make copies of pages including its children.

What just happened?

We've discovered some drag and drop functionality in concrete5. Whenever you want to restructure your page, these tools will help us achieve the task very quickly.

Splitting content into columns

As you've seen, you can use page types to choose between different page layouts. But what if your site looks like a newspaper—if it has more than 10 different layouts which are mostly unique? You could create a page type and template for each of them, but there's a smarter and easier way.

Time for action – creating a multi-column layout

To give your pages a multi-column layout, follow these steps:

1. Pick a page you've created in the previous section and open it.

2. Activate the edit mode by clicking on **Edit Page**.

3. When you click on **Add To Main** you should see the already familiar popup menu, but this time don't add a new block—select **Add Layout**.

4. After that, the following dialog should popup:

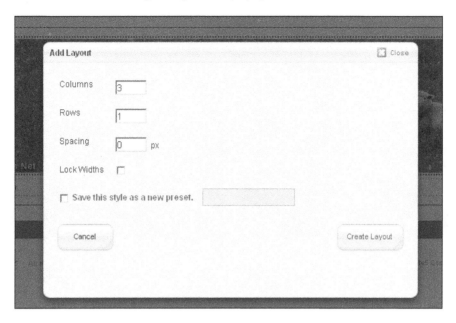

5. In this popup window, you've got several fields to enter values:

- **Columns**: Enter the number of columns your layout should have.
- **Rows**: Enter the number of rows you need for your table layout.
- **Spacing**: If you want to have some space between the columns, enter the value in pixels in this field.
- **Lock Widths**: Mark this checkbox if you want to avoid accidental changes to the column widths. You can unlock the layout at any time.
- **Save this style as a new preset**: If you need the same number of columns and rows several times, activate this and you'll be able to reuse it when adding a layout on another page.

6. Click on **Create Layout** when you're done.

7. The main area contains three sub-areas where you can add blocks:

8. The additional areas behave like any other areas, but there are some small differences if you look above the area:

Item	Explanation
	Click on this icon if you want to edit, delete or unlock/lock a layout.
	Columns in an unlocked layout can be resized by dragging these handles.

What just happened?

You have seen how easily you can split content into several columns. One area has been split into three columns to build a newspaper-like page. There's also a way to save these layouts as presets in case you want several pages to have the same column layout.

There are some blocks in each area which you reordered by using the move feature of concrete5. A feature that works not only with split areas, but areas in general.

With everything you've read so far you can create lots of different page layouts without having to write a single line of HTML code.

What you've seen so far should allow you to enter lots of different website content by using only very few tools.

 If there's some real content you want to add to your website, feel free to add it now. We won't remove any of the pages we've created, even when we create a new website layout!

Have a go hero – add more columns and blocks

Before you continue, try to add some blocks to the split areas. Try to build a newspaper like page with three columns, some content, and pictures. Since we're not working with real newspaper pages, you can also add some videos and show your grandparents what newspapers are going to look like in the future.

If you click on an existing block, you can select **Move** in the popup menu. concrete5 will then change the mode and enables block drag and drop functionality. You can even move blocks from one split area into another.

Scrapbook

When you build a website, there's always some content which is identical on several pages. For instance: A logo, an address, or a phone number if it appears on several pages. It's rather annoying if you manually have to make sure all the pages are updated, it takes quite some time and if you fail you'll quite likely get some complaints.

If you want to make things quick and dirty, put them in your PHP/HTML code and you're done. But you don't want to make things dirty, and luckily you don't have to because there's a scrapbook which is going to help you to get out of this misery.

Time for action – putting your addresses in a scrapbook

The following steps show you how to put your addresses in a scrapbook:

1. Log in to concrete5 and click on the **Dashboard** button. Select **Scrapbook** to see the following screen:

2. Open the **Global Scrapbook** by clicking on it.

3. Hit **Add Block to Scrapbook** to bring up the dialog with all installed blocks.

4. Select the **Content** block and enter your address and add it to the scrapbook. You should then see the additional block in the scrapbook with a small preview of its content:

5. You can rename blocks in the scrapbook by clicking on **Rename** to keep things organized.

6. Go back to your website by clicking on **Return to Website**.

7. Bring a page of your choice in the edit mode and click on **Add To Sidebar**. But instead of adding a new block, click on **Paste from Scrapbook**:

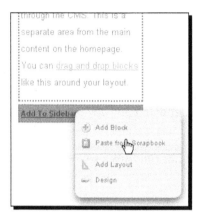

8. Select **Global Scrapbook** and click on the block you've previously added to the Dashboard. The block appears in the page like a normal block, with just one difference!

9. Click on the block you've just added and hit **Edit**; there's one small difference you can see on the next screenshot. concrete5 tells you that this is a global block where changes will affect all instances of this block throughout the site.

What just happened?

We've had a quick look at the scrapbook—a nice feature to manage blocks, used several times in your site. You can use it to globally manage every block available on your site.

If you build a website for a customer you can easily add all the global blocks in advance. The customer can then use the in-site editing system and won't have to learn how to use another tool and can quickly update several pages with one update.

Design and CSS

Some blocks already contain options to personalize the look or behavior of it, some blocks don't. However, concrete5 has a nice feature which uses CSS to customize the look of a block, even if the block developer didn't add any options to support custom colors, fonts, or anything like that.

You can see the following dialog to edit these, when you click on a block you've already added:

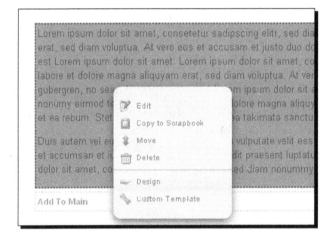

There are several options which apply different CSS rules to the selected block:

Time for action – styling your blocks

We would like to add an image to a page, but one that looks a bit emphasized, centered, and with a border around it.

1. Navigate to the page where you want to add the picture.

2. Go into the edit mode.

3. Add a new **Image** block:

4. Select **Choose Image** to bring up the file manager.

5. In the top right corner you can select a picture from your local hard disk. Hit **Upload** if you've selected the file you want to upload.

6. A small dialog appears where you could select another action to perform on the file:

> ❑ **Assign File Sets**: concrete5 doesn't use folders like a traditional file manager. Files can be assigned to one, several, or no sets.

> ❑ **Edit Properties**: Shows you some properties about the uploaded file. If you want to assign the file to a set, go for it, but it's just optional.

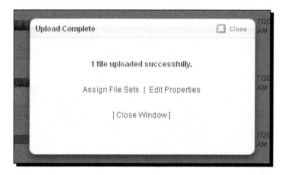

7. Close the dialog and you should see a new file in the manager:

8. Click on the file and hit **Choose** to select the file as the one you want to display in the image block.

9. Hit **Add** to insert the image block.

10. Click on the block after you've added it and select **Design**. You'll see some fields to add pre-defined CSS rules but also a text field in the **CSS** tab where more experienced CSS writers can add their own styles manually.

11. Go to the **Border** tab, set the **border style** to **solid** and width to **2px**. In the **Spacing** tab, enter 2px in each padding field and hit **Update**.

12. Our picture now has a black border. A simple design element you can add without any line of code. You can probably make it look even better.

What just happened?

We've added a picture block where we uploaded a new picture to the concrete5 file manager from our local hard disk.

We then added some CSS rules by using the concrete5 design feature to add a border around the picture.

There's a lot more you can do with the **Design** dialog, and here are some ideas:

- Add font styles, face, size, line height, and change the text color
- Insert a background color or picture
- Add different border styles to the block
- Put some space between the blocks by adding padding and margin
- Insert custom CSS rules or add an existing class to a block for more advanced CSS styling

The **Design** dialog is not only available on blocks but also on areas. If you click on **Add Area <Name>** you can find the **Design** item as well. This allows you to change all blocks within an area, for example, you can change the font face for a whole area.

Have a go hero – play around

We've covered a bunch of different things to manage your website's content. We didn't look at all the different tools, screens, or buttons but you soon realize that what you've seen should be enough for most situations.

But before we continue, try to make sure you're familiar with the following tools. Try to achieve these tasks:

◆ Add a page and edit some of its properties like the title, the URL, and so on.

◆ Each page can have a description which will be picked up by search engines. You can find it in the properties as well.

◆ Move and delete pages by using the **Sitemap** in the Dashboard.

◆ Add, remove, and re-order blocks.

◆ Upload, delete, and set properties for your files in the File Manager.

◆ Try to use these files in file, download, and videos blocks.

◆ Add a form with various controls and submit data that you'll later find in the Dashboard under the **Reports** section.

◆ Put blocks in the scrapbook.

Once you've successfully managed to execute these tasks you should be familiar with managing concrete5 page content.

Summary

We've already looked at everything you need to manage the content of your website. Using the features in this chapter allows you to create almost any page content you want. There are several things we did:

◆ We've added and edited blocks to update their content

◆ Worked with the sitemap to add, remove, and update pages to build a hierarchical page tree

◆ Split a page into several columns for a quick and easy layout creation

◆ We've had a look at the scrapbook to create a global block you can place on several pages but only have to update on one

◆ We used the design dialog to add a custom touch to an image block

3
Permissions

While concrete5 runs well without any special configuration, there are some parameters you can set to change the behavior of it to suit your needs. There are also several options to restrict access to your website.

We're going to look at the most important configurations you can make while adding a basic multiuser configuration which you can also use to build a simple extranet or member section on your website.

There's a section in the *Chapter 11, Deployment and Configuration* named configuration which might be helpful before you dive into this chapter. The following are the topics covered in the section:

- ◆ URL redirection, how does concrete5 handle requests on a website with several addresses
- ◆ How to change the language of the user interface in concrete5
- ◆ Some words about the cache options in concrete5 that might improve your website's performance

Basic permissions

When you run a website, you might want to have some personalized users with access to edit the page content, but without the rights to update all site settings. In this chapter, we're going to create a group, which you can assign to any number of users, if you want to give them edit access.

We're also going to create a section in your website, which is only visible to registered users. A first step towards an extranet! You can also use this method to hide certain pages on your website from your parents.

Adding users and groups

Users usually come and go; to keep the handling as easy as possible, we're going to create a group for everything, even if there's just one user in it.

Time for action – adding groups

Carry out the following steps to add a group:

1. Log in to concrete5 and go to the **Dashboard**.

2. Select **Users and Groups** in the navigation on the left.

3. The screen to create new groups is straightforward, as shown in the following screenshot:

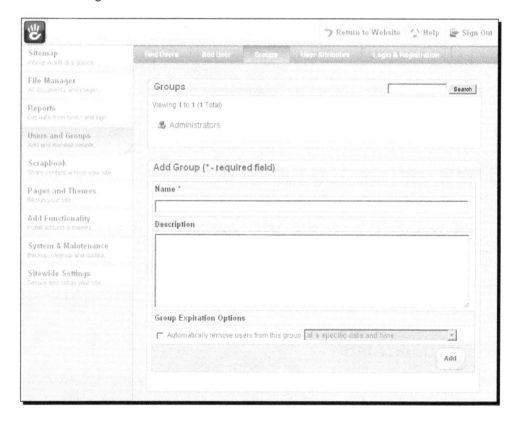

4. Enter a group named Editors in the **Name** field. Click on **Add** to create the group.

5. Create another group named Members, which we'll use to manage the users with access to our secret website section.

What just happened?

We created two new groups, which we'll use during the process of building a small community website. One is for the users with access to manage the website content and another is for members who only get access to the normal website view without any access to the dashboard or in-site editing toolbar.

Group expiration options

You might have noticed the expiration settings at the bottom (see the preceding screenshot) when you created the groups. We don't need them at this point, but they can be quite handy. Imagine you want to build a website where you sell subscriptions. How do you make sure people have to pay after a certain period has passed by? You just set an expiration option and you're done! There are two different ways to do that, which are as follows:

- **Automatically remove users from this group** at a specific date and time: Enter a fixed date the members should be removed or deactivated from the group.

- **Automatically remove users from this group once a certain amount of time has passed**: Set a period after which the members of the group have to be removed or deactivated.

Time for action – adding users

1. Go to the **Dashboard** and select **Users and Groups**.

2. Click on **Add User** in the top navigation and you see a screen similar to the following screenshot:

3. The first three fields are mandatory. Enter your user credentials for the account you want to use as an editor in **Username**, **Password** and **Email Address**. Tick **Editors** at the bottom to assign the user the necessary group.

4. Click on **Create User**.

5. Create another user you want to use as a test member for your extranet. You should now have three users, as shown in the following screenshot:

What just happened?

We've created two new users with restricted permissions to edit the page and view a protected section we're going to create. They are now visible when you have a look at the user section in the dashboard. In case the list gets bigger, concrete5 offers several tools, including the following:

- A search box to search after a username or e-mail address
- Filters to display users belonging to one or more groups
- An Excel export if you want to process the user data manually

User attributes

When you created the new account, you probably saw the box named **Registration Data**. Almost every website has different needs; while you need a username and password for all of them, you probably don't need the same user attributes on every site.

concrete5 has a flexible and extendable attribute system allowing you to create and assign attributes not just to users but also pages and files.

During the account creation, you saw a few default attributes about message processing created during the installation process. We don't need them at this point, but in case you want to keep track of more data about your users, create attributes and you've got a flexible system to manage your user data. We're going to add page attributes, which work the same way as user attributes in *Chapter 5, Create your Own Theme.*

Sitemap and file manager permissions

By default, a group has no rights. To give a group access to edit your website's pages, we have to grant them more rights. First, let's make sure that they get access to the sitemap.

Time for action – assigning sitemap permissions

Carry out the following for assigning sitemap permissions:

1. Go to the **Dashboard** and select **Sitemap**.

2. Select **Access** in the top navigation.

3. Our groups aren't visible yet; click on **Add Group or User** and select **Editors** in the dialog.

4. Check the **Yes** radio button next to **Access Sitemap and Page Search** to give your Editors access to the sitemap. It should look like the following screenshot:

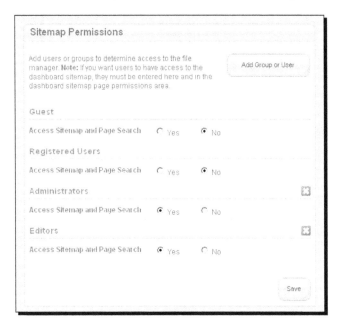

What just happened?

We've granted our editors the right to access the sitemap. This allows them to move and delete pages using the in-site editing toolbar. They don't have access to the dashboard sitemap yet though. You'll find an explanation about granting partial access to the dashboard later in this chapter.

Now that you've allowed your editors to access the sitemap, you have to grant them access to the file manager. They need to be able to add pictures and files to the pages they create, don't they?

Time for action – granting file manager permissions

1. Open the Dashboard and select **File Manager**.

2. Navigate to **Access**.

3. Click on **Add Group or User** and select **Editors** and the following screen pops up:

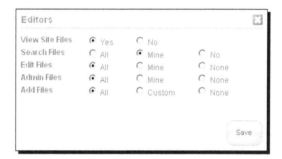

4. Hit **Save** to confirm the changes.

What just happened?

You granted all members of **Editors** access to the file manager. This allows them to upload, delete, and use the files within the pages.

By default, they are only going to see their own files. This can be handy if you, the admin, want to upload system files that a normal user isn't supposed to see. However, if you want to manage the page content using the admin account as well, you might have to allow any user to see all files. In this case, you simply set **Search Files** to **All**.

Granting edit access

We've got two new users, each of them a member of a group. This is the basic structure we're going to use for all our permissions. However, they don't have more rights than a user without any assigned group.

The basic permission mode has a simple screen where you can grant a group the necessary rights to edit pages.

As shown in the following screenshot, go to **Dashboard |Sitewide Settings |Access** and enable the checkbox for **Editors** to grant them the edit right:

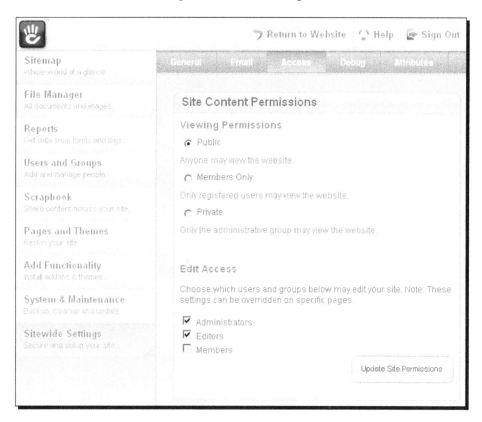

Managing edit access on a page by page basis

By activating edit access for all members of **Editors**, we allowed them to edit every page in our website. Internally, concrete5 assigns permissions to each page, even with the global setting that we just enabled.

Due to this detailed execution, we can manage permissions on a more precise level, if necessary. You can find the actual permissions concrete5 assigned if you navigate to the sitemap and click on a page in the tree and select **Set Permissions** as shown in the following screenshot:

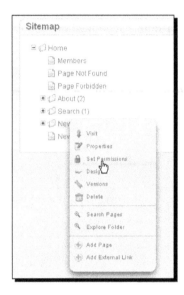

The dialog is split into two different parts; on the bottom, you can see all the groups allowed to edit the page, and on top there's a list of groups able to view this page.

As we globally activated edit access to the group Editors, the checkbox for this **Editors** group is ticked for every page by default. However, if you want to revoke the edit right for one page, go ahead and uncheck the checkbox in this dialog, as shown in the following screenshot:

Creating a protected website section

You may have some secret information that you would like to put on the website that only certain members should see. This can be handled with a password protected section.

Time for action – creating a protected website

Carry out the following steps:

1. Navigate to **Dashboard | Sitemap** and create a new page named `VIP`.

2. Click on the new page and select **Set Permissions**.

3. Uncheck the checkbox next to **Guest** in **Who can view this page**.

4. Tick the checkbox next to **Members** in **Who can view this page**.

5. Click on **Save**.

What just happened?

We removed the right for guests to access our VIP page but allowed members to access it. When you log out, you won't see the VIP page anymore:

You can send users belonging to the members group to the same login page you're using when you want to edit your website: `http://localhost/login/`. Use the member account you've created earlier to log in and a new page will be visible:

That's everything you need to do if you want to protect a page. Every block you place in such a page won't be accessible to users who aren't logged in. A secret guestbook or a personal poem—you decide who gets access to it!

Task permissions

While it should probably suffice to grant file and sitemap permissions in most situations, you might get a big project where you want to split up the task with an even higher granularity. There's another screen in concrete5 where you can manage a few more task permissions.

Time for action – setting task permissions

1. Go to the **Dashboard** and select **Sitewide Settings** in the left navigation.

2. Activate the **Access** tab.

3. Click on **Click here to modify other permissions** in the **Other Permissions** box.

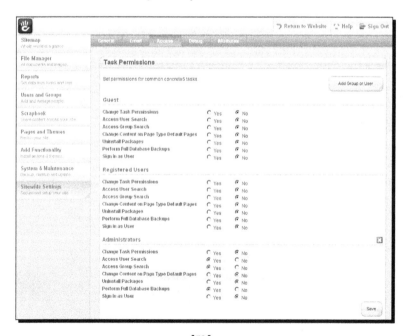

4. Manually added groups aren't listed by default; they have to be added first. Click on **Add Group or User** and select your group in the dialog.

5. We only activate **Change Content on Page Type Default Pages** and **Perform Full Database Backups**. Backups almost never hurt and updating default blocks for a page type can be quite powerful for an editor, but also a bit dangerous. If your editors aren't people who work carefully, you might want to skip that option.

What just happened?

We assigned two task permissions to our group Editors to give them a bit more power over your concrete5 site. If you think you'll need more groups, different task permissions, go ahead; nothing in the next chapter depends on them.

Dashboard access

The permissions we've set should work for most situations, but as always, there might be an exception where an editor would like to see the hierarchical page tree in the dashboard to get a better overview of the website.

It would be nice if we could allow editors to access the dashboard, but only certain parts of it. We don't want them to delete our users or change the sitewide settings. It takes a few clicks, but we can allow our users to access only a few items in the dashboard.

Time for action – granting partial dashboard access

1. Go to the **Dashboard** and click on **Sitemap**.

2. In the Sitemap, tick the checkbox **Show System Pages** to display the Dashboard pages in the Sitemap.

3. Select the **Dashboard** page and click on **Set Permissions**.

4. Tick the checkbox for **Editors** in the upper part, **Who can view this page?**

5. Click on **Save**.

concrete5 has inherited new permissions for all sub pages of the dashboard page. This means that we are granted access to every item in the dashboard, which is exactly what we didn't want to do. While the inheritance is usually quite handy if you want to change the permissions, in this case it leads to a few more clicks. We have to revoke the rights from all the dashboard sub pages that we don't want the editors to have access to.

6. Expand the dashboard page by clicking on the small plus icon in front of the page name.

7. Expand the Sitemap as well.

8. Click on the subpage **Access** and click on **Set Permissions**.

9. Uncheck the checkbox for **Editors** in the **Who can view this page** section.

10. Do the same for these pages underneath **Dashboard**:

- ❏ **File Manager | Attributes**
- ❏ **File Manager | Access**
- ❏ **Reports | Logs**
- ❏ **Users and Groups**
- ❏ **Scrapbook**
- ❏ **Pages and Themes**
- ❏ **Add Functionality**
- ❏ **System Maintenance**
- ❏ **Sitewide Settings**

What just happened?

As long as you didn't get a tennis elbow from all those clicks, you should now have a dashboard which is partially accessible by your editors. When you log in to concrete5 with your editor account, you'll only see a part of the dashboard, as shown in the following screenshot:

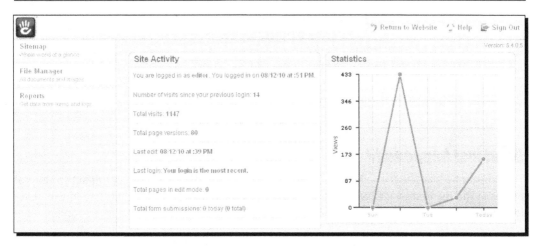

You are, of course, free to modify the list of pages we revoked from the group; the scrapbook for example, could be quite handy for a power editor.

Advanced permission mode

The permissions you've seen in the previous section should be enough for a lot of websites. However, sometimes you want to restrict the access even more. What if you wanted to achieve the following things?

♦ Restrict the blocks that a user can use

♦ Make a page visible only during a certain time period

♦ Get area and block specific control over your content

You haven't seen any of it, but everything is possible; you just have to activate the advanced permission mode.

Time for action – activating the advanced permission mode

Carry out the following steps:

1. Open your configuration file `config/site.php` in your text editor.

2. Insert this line `define('PERMISSIONS_MODEL', 'advanced');` within the PHP tags. The file should look like the following:

```php
<?php
  define('DB_SERVER', 'localhost');
  define('DB_USERNAME', 'concrete5');
  define('DB_PASSWORD', 'concrete5');
```

```
define('DB_DATABASE', 'concrete5');
define('BASE_URL', 'http://localhost');
define('DIR_REL', '');
define('PASSWORD_SALT', 'R3nAjizpVw3AbleCFCuQIzNACYvnxoq');

define('PERMISSIONS_MODEL', 'advanced');
?>
```

What just happened?

The constant PERMISSIONS_MODEL is set to advanced, which has a direct impact to several places in the user interface. We're going to look at the changes this constant had in the next few steps.

One quick preview: When you open the permissions dialog for a page, you'll see a completely different dialog with a lot more options. You can control each action which can be executed on a page for every group you've created:

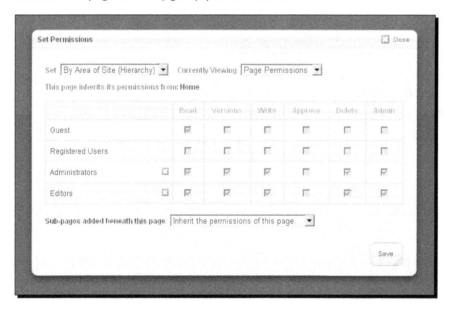

In the preceding screen, you can specify the source of the permissions. You can also select **Manually** in the **Set** drop-down, if you want to override the permissions for a certain page only. You can switch between different modes by changing the value in **Currently Viewing**:

- ◆ **Page Permissions**: If you choose **Manually** for this section, you're able to specify every action a certain group is allowed to execute. You can specify who's allowed to update a page, approve a page modification, and so on.
- ◆ **Sub-Page Permissions**: Specify the page types a user can add. See section *Sub page permissions*, later in this chapter.
- ◆ **Timed Released Settings**: Restrict the time a page is visible. More details are provided in *Time based page visibility* section (the following section).

You can also specify what permissions a new page should get by choosing the option which suits your needs at the bottom in **Sub-pages added beneath this page**. There are the following two options:

- ◆ **Inherit the permissions of this page**: Copies the permissions from the current page to the new subpage.
- ◆ **Inherit page type default permissions**: You can specify default permissions on a page type, if you open the page type defaults using the dashboard: **Dashboard | Pages and Themes | Page Types | Defaults**.

Time based page visibility

There are lots of situations where you might want to create a page but keep it hidden for a while. Some publications should be visible on a certain date only and some offers should only be visible for a specific time.

You can do all of this with a few clicks, but only if you've activated the advanced permission mode.

Time for action – setting time based page visibility

Carry out the following steps:

1. Make sure that you've activated the advanced permission mode.

2. Go to the Sitemap and click on the page that you want to appear during a specified period only.

3. Click on **Set Permissions** once again.

4. Change **Currently Viewing** to **Timed Release Settings** and you should see the following screen:

5. Select **Manually** in the top left drop-down **Set**; the controls should be enabled now.

6. Enable the two checkboxes in the row of **Guest** and specify the period between the page is supposed to be accessible.

7. Click on **Save**.

What just happened?

By enabling the advanced permission mode, you've gotten the possibility to add timed release settings to your pages. We restricted the guest access for a page. This could be used if you wanted to give paying members early access to your content.

It also helps you if you need several days to prepare a page. Create the page, add some content, send a link to management and once you've got the confirmation, go ahead, and remove the timed setting.

Subpage permissions

concrete5 also allows you to restrict the page types a user is allowed to add as a subpage.

Time for action – setting sub-page permissions

Carry out the following steps:

1. In the same dialog (refer the preceding screenshot), change **Currently Viewing** to **Sub-Page Permissions** to get a list with groups and page types, as shown in the following screenshot:

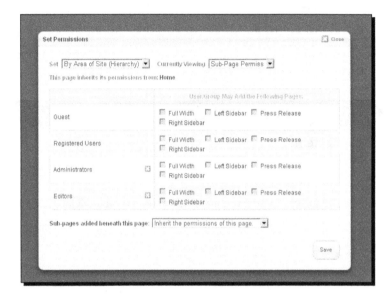

2. Switch the value in the drop-down at **Set** to **Manually**.

3. Select the page types you want your Editors to be able to add as subpages.

4. Click on **Save** to apply the new settings.

What just happened?

If you have a person who's only responsible for managing press releases, they only need one page type. By using the advanced permission mode, you can make sure that they don't see and care about the other pages types.

This is useful if your website gets bigger and has lots of page types. However, keep in mind that it might help your end users, but also increases the effort necessary to manage the website.

Block based permissions

While the advanced permissions give you a lot of power over page permissions, you also get more control over areas and blocks. You can now set permissions on block level for an extremely detailed management of permissions.

However, be careful when you use this feature. You might want to think about it twice, as it gets quite complicated to manage permissions on such a detailed level. Forget where you specified block permissions and you'll end up fixing and digging around your website very quickly.

We are going to use it anyways. In this case, we're adding a simple content block to inform our members about the new protected website section we created earlier.

Time for action – using block permissions

Carry out the following steps:

1. Make sure that you've enabled the advanced permission mode.

2. Navigate to the home page and start editing the page by clicking on **Edit Page**.

3. Add a new content block to the sidebar where you'd like to inform your members about the new section, as shown in the following screenshot:

4. Due to our deliberate understatement, we'd like to make sure that guests cannot see the new content block. Click on the block again and click on **Set Permissions**, as shown in the following screenshot:

5. In the dialog showing up, simply uncheck the checkbox for Guests and click on **Update**, as shown in the following screenshot:

What just happened?

We revoked the right for guests to see a single content block. This works with any block in concrete5, not just content blocks.

But again, think about this. Using such a high level of permissions is probably more difficult to manage than you think.

Area based permissions

The advanced permission mode also adds permissions to areas where you can specify the blocks allowed to be used in an area. If your website has grown over the time, you might have installed lots of blocks which can be confusing to new users. While power users might need all blocks, the person who manages the news is probably happy with very few blocks.

Let's make sure that our editors only have access to the blocks they really need.

Time for action – restricting allowed blocks for an area

Carry out the following steps:

1. Make sure that the advanced permission mode has been activated.

2. Navigate to your home page and enter the edit mode.

3. Click on **Add to Sidebar** and select **Set Permissions**, as shown in the following screenshot:

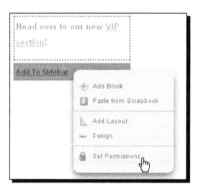

4. In the dialog, you'll see your default groups and every block including the actions read, write, and delete, as shown in the following screenshot:

5. By default, the editor group is allowed to add every block. Simply remove those you don't want your editors to use and confirm the changes by clicking on **Update**.

What just happened?

By using the area permissions, we've hidden some blocks from our editors. This can make the editing of concrete5 even easier.

If you're building a site for an inexperienced computer user, use this feature to hide some of the complexity and even a computer newbie is going to like working with you and concrete5.

Pop quiz – permissions in concrete5

1. Which features are only available when you activate the advanced permission mode?

   ❑ Area permissions to restrict the blocks which can be added to an area

   ❑ Grant rights to the file manager

   ❑ Block permissions to specify who can read, write, and delete a specific block

   ❑ Page permissions to hide a certain page from a user group

   ❑ Time based page visibility to hide a page for a specified time

2. How do you have to activate the advanced permission mode?

    ❏ Checkbox in the **Dashboard** in the section **Sitewide Settings**

    ❏ Configuration line in `config/site.php`

    ❏ Configuration line in `config.php`

Summary

In this chapter you've learnt how to configure your concrete5 website.

◆ We looked at permissions and created users without administration rights to edit the website.

◆ We've used this as well to create a VIP section on the website which is only visible to members of your website.

◆ We've activated the advanced permission mode to get access to a few more features allowing you to control almost every aspect of your site in terms of permissions.

◆ We then looked at permissions and created users without administration rights to edit the website. We've used this as a base to create a VIP section in your website, which is only visible to members of your website. In case your site has lots of different users—we've activated the advanced permission mode to get access to a few more features allowing you to control almost every aspect of your site in terms of permissions.

4
Add-ons

concrete5 ships with a bunch of add-ons to build a basic site without adding any additional components. However, the deeper you get into concrete5 the more you'll realize that you want more features.

Thankfully, there's a marketplace with some free and some commercial add-ons to extend concrete5 without having any development skills.

We are going to look at the different add-ons to learn about their structure to get a first impression of how an add-on looks under the hood. Even if you don't intend to build your own blocks or packages, this helps you to understand the basics of concrete5 and makes it easier to help and support your customers.

What's an add-on?

A concrete5 add-on is basically a directory with a bunch of files. Everything you need is located within a single directory. For most add-ons, you don't have to manually execute any tasks, which you'll later see when we install an add-on.

There are different kinds of add-ons; we'll quickly look at all of them, but let's install an add-on first.

Installing add-ons from the marketplace

If everything works fine, you can use the dashboard to install new add-ons without ever leaving your site.

Time for action – installing an add-on

Carry out the following steps to install an add-on:

1. Go to your dashboard and click on **Add Functionality**.

2. Before you can access the marketplace, you have to connect to the concrete5.org community. Click on **Connect to Community**. You're redirected to a screen where you can enter the details about your site.

3. Enter the information about your site. No one is going to see this information; it's only supposed to make it easier for you to manage your sites. You also have to create a concrete5.org community account if you haven't done it already.

This has nothing to do with the accounts you've already created within your site. This is an account for concrete5.org. You can use one account to connect all your sites to the marketplace; you can also use it to access the support forums on concrete5.org. If you haven't created an account before, click on **Create a new account on concrete5.org** and enter all the requested data, as shown in the following screenshot.

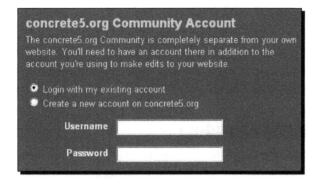

4. After your site has been connected with the marketplace, you get back to the screen which shows the installed add-ons. Click on **More Add-Ons** to browse the marketplace add-ons, as shown in the following screenshot:

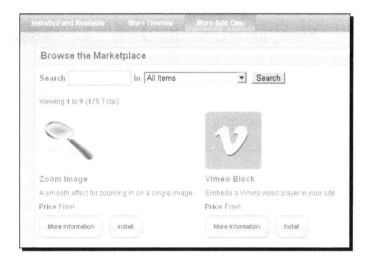

5. Look for an add-on you like and click on **Install**.

Time for action – removing an add-on

Carry out the following steps if you want to remove an add-on:

1. You don't like the add-on you just installed? Go to **Add Functionality** again and locate the previously installed add-on. Click on the **Edit** button next to the add-on.

2. At the bottom, you can find a button **Uninstall Package**. Click on it and the add-on is no longer listed under the installed add-ons; it's now listed on the right where all installable add-ons can be found.

What just happened?

By connecting your site to the concrete5.org marketplace, you gained direct access to all add-ons uploaded to the marketplace. We've installed an add-on and also removed it. The process to install a theme works the same way; click on **Add Functionality** but this time locate **More Themes** and pick a layout.

Manually installing an add-on

The automatic installation process depends on a few PHP modules, such as cURL which if missing will make it impossible to install an add-on using the preceding procedure. If you aren't sure whether cURL is enabled on your server, go to *Chapter 11, Deployment and Configuration* and look at the *Time for action – get PHP information* section. Once you've created the file described in that section, you can see some information about cURL if it's installed. In the case that it isn't, contact your host and ask if they can install it.

Time for action – manually installing an add-on

Carry out the following steps to install an add-on manually:

1. Go to `http://www.concrete5.org` and click on **Marketplace** at the top.

2. Find the add-on that you want to install.

3. Click on the **Download** button at the bottom.

4. On the next screen, click on **Download Now**.

5. Extract the downloaded ZIP file into the `packages` folder of your concrete5 site. If you're working with a default XAMPP setup, the folder is `c:\xampplite\htdocs\packages`.

6. Go back to your site's dashboard.

7. Click on **Add Functionality**.

8. In the right column underneath **Downloaded and Ready to Install** should be the add-on you've downloaded. Click on **Install** and it will be ready to use.

What just happened?

By manually downloading and extracting the add-on, you've avoided the need for a few PHP modules which aren't installed on every host.

Every add-on from the marketplace is wrapped into a package, no matter whether it's a theme, block, or just a template. This means you don't have to worry about the add-on type; just install themes as a package and you'll be fine! Don't worry too much about the different add-on types at the moment, as we're going to talk about them later in this chapter.

It's also less likely that you'll run into file system permission problems because you're moving the files on your own. There are a few hints about moving your site to a Linux server in *Chapter 11*, *Deployment and Configuration* where we also quickly look at the file permissions. The user account the web server uses has usually only very few rights to reduce the potential security risk. However, this can also make it more difficult for web applications to execute certain commands on the server, such as downloading and extracting files.

Theme

A theme is responsible for the look of your website. By default, there are three themes you can choose. You can see them when you navigate to **Dashboard** | **Pages and Themes**, as shown in the following screenshot:

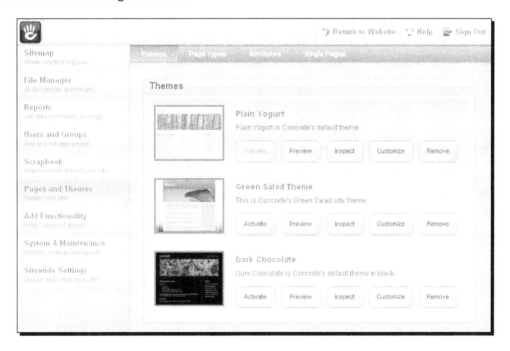

A theme isn't restricted to a certain layout structure like a portal. concrete5 themes can be built using any HTML and CSS code you want. You can even create your JavaScript files on the fly. You therefore find lots of different layouts and whatever you'd like to build; there are pretty much no limits.

You can activate a theme by clicking on **Activate**. Confirm the activation on the next screen and your website changes its layout immediately. If you're working on an active site, you might want to hit **Preview** first to see how your page is going to look with the new theme.

Parts of a theme

We're going to create a theme in the next chapter, but before we start creating our own layout, let's look at the way pages and their page types are organized in concrete5.

When you click on **Inspect**, you'll see a dialog like the following screenshot where some elements of the theme will be displayed:

Each theme contains at least one template, the `default.php` file which will be used for a page type without a template. The following illustration shows you the difference between a page type and a template:

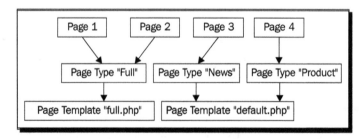

Each page has one page type. If there's a file in the theme with the same name as the page type, it will be used and therefore has its own layout. For every page type without a matching file in the theme, `default.php` will be used. This means that several page types can share one layout. In the preceding illustration, **News** and **Product** both have the same layout.

Theme file structure

Not every theme contains the same files but there are some files which you'll find in most of the themes. We're going to create a complete theme in the next chapter but just to give you a first impression about the basic structure of a theme without going into all the details. This can be helpful to understand concrete5 a little bit better, even if you don't intend to create your own theme.

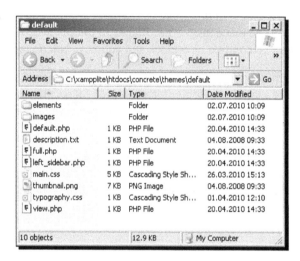

Most themes contain more or less the same files; the preceding screenshot shows you the most common files. Here are same files along with a short explanation:

- `Elements`: This directory usually contains two files, which are `header.php` and `footer.php`. They are used to make sure you don't have to add a header and footer to every template you create. They are optional though.

- `Images`: Most themes use a few pictures; put them in this directory.

- `Default.php`: This is the default file used by concrete5 to render your page.

- `Description.txt`: This file is used when you install a theme, and it contains the name and a short description.

- `Full.php`: This is like `default.php` a template, but only used by pages of the type full.

- `Left_sidebar.php`: Another template for the page type left sidebar.

- **Main.css**: The CSS file in concrete5 themes is usually called `main.css`. You aren't forced to call your CSS file `main.css` though.

- **Thumbnail.png**: Only displayed in the dashboard to make it easier to identify your theme.

- **Typography.css**: A second CSS file used by the page but also by the content block for a proper preview of your text.

- **View.php**: A special template used for single pages which you have to create programmatically.

Blocks

We've already seen a few blocks in the previous chapters. In case you forgot: A block is basically an element you can place in an area. Thanks to the really extensible architecture of concrete5, it's quite easy to create a new block and add new functionality to your website.

Blocks are just like anything in concrete5 built using the **Model-View-Controller** (**MVC**) pattern. This makes sure that every element in concrete5 follows the same structure. A developer who builds extensions for concrete5 should have experience with object oriented programming and the MVC pattern.

Understanding the MVC pattern isn't very difficult but helps pretty much any developer. It basically makes sure that the layout (view) is in a file, split apart from the logic (controller) and the data (model). You can find more information about the pattern on Wikipedia: http://en.wikipedia.org/wiki/Model_View_Controller.

Block structure

What files does a block need?

This goes a bit deeper but might still be handy for a non-developer to know. Just knowing where the files are located can help you to make some minor modifications to a block.

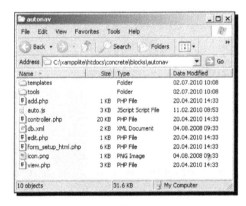

The preceding screenshot shows you the files a basic block has, and these are their purposes:

- `Templates`: A block can have different layouts. A picture gallery might use a pop-up to display the picture or some JavaScript for a more dynamic design. `Templates` is where you'd find these block layouts.

- `Tools`: Some blocks use AJAX in their interface. Such AJAX scripts are usually located in this directory.

- `Add.php`: This is the file used for the block dialog when you add a new instance of a block.

- `Auto.js`: An automatically added JavaScript file when editing your block.

- `Controller.php`: This is where all the magic happens—processing your data, converting your input, saving it to the database, and so on.

- `Db.xml`: Most blocks have their own tables; you can find the table definition in this file.

- `Edit.php`: When you edit an existing block, this is the file used for the interface.

- `Form_setup_html.php`: As most blocks work almost the same way, whether you add or edit them, they share parts of their interfaces by moving them into this file.

- `Icon.png`: A little icon 16x16 pixels used in the block list when choosing a block to add.

- `View.php`: This file renders the block output.

Packages

A package is basically a container for all elements. You can use it to wrap a theme, resources, and blocks into a single package. This is mostly useful if you intend to build a big extension where all the elements are connected together.

By using a package, you make add-ons easier to handle and install. You can also make the installation process a bit more solid by extending the package's installer method to check the requirements.

You can easily recognize a package by looking at its structure, which is shown in the following screenshot:

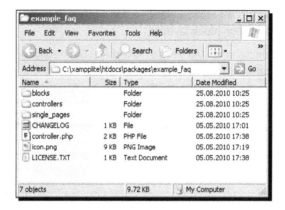

There are several indications telling you that you're looking at a package and not just a block or theme:

- There's a subdirectory called `blocks` or `theme` or any of the directories you can find in the root of your site.
- The controller is the only PHP file you can find in the root. A block would at least need `edit.php` and `add.php`.

 Every add-on in the marketplace is built as a package to make the handling as easy as possible, even if there's just a single block in it.

Pop quiz – what's a package?

concrete5 allows you to use packages. What's their purpose?

- Wrap different elements like themes and blocks into a single element for easy handling and deployment.
- Prepare your concrete5 site for deployment to another server.
- Creating an installer for your extension where you can check the requirements and create concrete5 objects your extension needs to work.
- Preparing a concrete5 extension to be published in the official concrete5 marketplace.

Summary

While there's a lot more you can extend in concrete5 by using a package, blocks and themes are the ones you'll most likely need on a daily basis when you work with concrete5. A package could contain controllers, single pages, events, and a lot more to extend almost anything you want without touching the core. You haven't reached the end after you've gone through themes and blocks!

We've had a quick look at the marketplace; you should know how to install add-ons automatically and also manually.

You should have a basic understanding about the structure of themes, blocks, and packages. We're going to cover all of them in the next few chapters, but make sure you know what an add-on directory looks like. Following the same pattern as every concrete5 developer keeps the process simple and clean for everybody.

5
Creating Your Own Theme

In this chapter, we're going to change the layout of the site we've created. To achieve this, we will convert an HTML file into a concrete5 theme. This means that we have to replace and insert a few lines of PHP code to make things a bit more dynamic. However, you'll see that the basic conversion process is rather easy and quick, creating a concrete5 theme does only require very little HTML skills and almost no time.

Some code snippets are just modifications to other snippets in this chapter. If you want to re-create the theme code on your own, you have to follow each step and follow the instructions precisely. If you're in a hurry, at the end of the chapter you'll find a link where you can download the finished theme.

The new layout

Before we start creating a concrete5 theme we need a layout. In this book, we're going to use a simple layout without any pictures to keep the code as short as possible—it's about concrete5 not about HTML and CSS.

If you don't have the time for an exercise, you can use your own layout. With good knowledge of the basic technologies underneath concrete5, you should be able to amend the instructions in this chapter to match your own layout. If you don't feel very comfortable working with PHP you should probably use the printed HTML code in this chapter.

First, a screenshot—this is what the site is going to look like once we've finished our theme:

While this layout isn't very pretty, it has an easy structure: Navigation on top and a big content where we can insert any kind of block we want. If you're using your own layout, try to use one with a simple structure, navigation on top or on the left with one big place for the content, and try to avoid Flash. It is possible to use Flash and even a dynamic Flash menu can be created with some programming knowledge but that's beyond the scope of this book.

The HTML code

Let's have a look at the HTML code:

```
<!DOCTYPE html PUBLIC "-//W3C//DTD XHTML 1.0 Transitional//EN"
"http://www.w3.org/TR/xhtml1/DTD/xhtml1-transitional.dtd">
<html xmlns="http://www.w3.org/1999/xhtml" xml:lang="en" lang="en">
<head>

<title>Concrete5 Theme</title>
<meta http-equiv="Content-Type" content="text/html;charset=utf-8" />
<style type="text/css" media="screen">@import "main.css";</style>

</head>
<body>

<div id="wrapper">
    <div id="page">
```

```
<div id="header_line_top"></div>
<div id="header">
<ul class="nav-dropdown">
<li><a href="#">Home</a></li>
<li><a href="#">Test</a></li>
<li><a href="#">About</a></li>
</ul>
</div>
<div id="header_line_bottom"></div>
<div id="content">
<p>
Paragraph 1
</p>

<p>
Paragraph 2
</p>

<p>
Paragraph 3
</p>
</div>
<div id=»footer_line_top»></div>
<div id=»footer»></div>
<div id=»footer_line_bottom»></div>
</div>
</div>

</body>
</html>
```

There are three highlighted lines in the preceding code:

+ The CSS import—to keep the layout instructions separated from the HTML elements, we've got all the CSS rules in a different file named main.css. This is also how almost all concrete5 themes are built.

+ The header block contains the navigation. As we're going to apply some styles to it, make sure it has its own ID. Using an ID also improves the performance when using CSS and JavaScript to access an element, as an ID is unique.

+ The same applies to the content block. Make sure it has a unique ID.

Most web technologies we use nowadays are standardized in one way or another. Currently, the most important organization is W3C. They also offer tools to validate your code.

 Checking your code is never a bad idea. Navigate to `http://validator.w3.org/` and enter the address of the website you want to check or in this case. As your website isn't accessible by the public, click on **Validate by Direct Input** and paste the HTML code to see if there are any mistakes. While it should be fairly easy to produce valid HTML code, things are a bit tricky with CSS. Due to some old browser bugs, you're often forced to use invalid CSS rules. There's often a way to rebuild the layout to avoid some invalid rules but sometimes this isn't the case; you won't be doomed if something isn't 100% valid but you're on the safer side if it is.

CSS rules

As mentioned earlier, all CSS rules are placed in a file named `main.css`. Let's have a look at all CSS rules you have to put in our CSS file:

```
/* global HTML tag rules */
html, body, div, pre, form, fieldset, input, h1, h2, h3, h4, h5, h6,
p, textarea, ul, ol, li, dl, dt, dd, blockquote, th, td {
margin: 0;
padding: 0;
}
p {
margin: 5px 0px 15px 0px;
}
html {
height: 100%;
}
body {
background-color: #989898;
height: 100%;
}

/* layout rules */
#wrapper {
margin: 0 auto;
width: 980px;
text-align: left;
padding-top: 35px;
}

#page {
background: #FFFFFF;
```

```
float: left;
width: 960px;
padding: 5px;
-moz-box-shadow: 0 0 15pxblack;
-webkit-box-shadow: 0 0 15pxblack;
box-shadow: 0 0 15pxblack;
border-radius: 10px;
}
/* header */
#header {
background: #262626;
border-radius: 10px 10px 0px 0px;
height: 75px;
}
#header_line_top {
background: #262626;
height: 0px;
}
#header_line_bottom {
background: #e64116;
height: 3px;
}
/* content */
#content {
min-height: 300px;
padding: 30px;
color: #1E1E1E;

font-family: verdana, helvetica, arial;
font-size: 13px;
line-height: 22px;
}
/* footer */
#footer {
background: #262626;
height: 75px;
border-radius: 0px 0px 10px 10px;
}
#footer_line_top {
background: #e64116;
height: 3px;
}
#footer_line_bottom {
background: #262626;
```

```
   height: 0px;
   }
   /* header navigation */
   #header ul{
   margin: 0px;
   padding: 20px;
   }
   #header ulli {
   float: left;
   list-style-type: none;
   }
   #header ulli a {
   margin-right: 20px;
   display: block;
   padding: 6px 15px 6px 15px;
   color: #ccc;
   text-decoration: none;
   font-family: verdana, helvetica, arial;
   }
   #header ulli a:hover {
   color: white;
   }
```

As already mentioned, there are situations where the CSS file won't validate. The preceding code is such an example, but not due to bugs in old browsers, but rather due to new features not officially available in all browsers. Browser vendors often implement features before they're standardized. They often start with a prefix like -webkit or -moz. At this point it's a decision you have to make: either use the new features and make the CSS file invalid, or don't.

In this case, It doesn't really hurt to use some of the new CSS3 features. Just make sure you don't depend on them; the layout we're using looks a bit different when you look at it using a browser like Internet Explorer 6.0, you won't see any shadows but the layout still works.

Converting HTML and CSS to a concrete5 theme

We've got our HTML and CSS files, so now we want them to be part of a new concrete5 theme with two editable areas, one for the content and one for the header. We ignore the footer for now.

Time for action – creating the concrete5 theme header

Carry out the following steps:

1. In the `themes` directory, create a new directory named `c5book`, but any other name is fine as long as you're using letters and underscores and avoid the special characters available on your keyboard.

2. Create a thumbnail 120 x 90 pixels of your site and save it as `thumbnail.png` within your theme directory.

3. Create a file named `description.txt` in the new directory by using a text editor, such as Notepad.

4. Open the file and enter the name of the theme in the first line and the description on the second line. Its content should look like the following:

    ```
    c5book Theme
    Concrete5 Theme by Remo Laubacher
    ```

5. Save and close the file. You should have a structure like the one shown in the following screenshot:

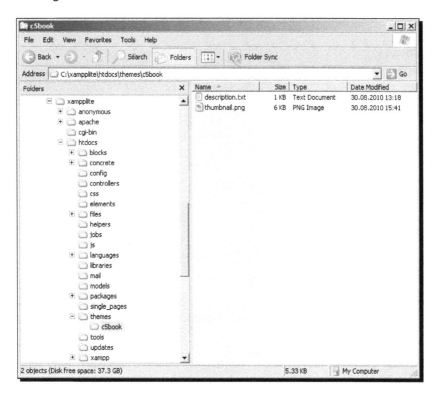

6. As we're going to create several page layouts sharing the same header and footer, let's create a directory named `elements` for these common files.

7. Within `elements`, create a file named `header.php` and insert all the preceding HTML code, including the `DIV` element with the ID `header_line_bottom`.

```php
<?php defined('C5_EXECUTE') or die( _("Access Denied.")); ?>
<!DOCTYPE html PUBLIC "-//W3C//DTD XHTML 1.0 Transitional//EN"
"http://www.w3.org/TR/xhtml1/DTD/xhtml1-transitional.dtd">
<html xmlns="http://www.w3.org/1999/xhtml" xml:lang="en"
lang="en">
<head>

<title>Concrete5 Theme</title>
<meta http-equiv="Content-Type" content="text/html;charset=utf-8"
/>

<link rel="stylesheet" media="screen" type="text/css" href="<?php
echo $this->getStyleSheet('main.css')?>" />
<link rel="stylesheet" media="screen" type="text/css" href="<?php
echo $this->getStyleSheet('typography.css')?>" />

<?php  Loader::element('header_required'); ?>

</head>
<body>

<div id="wrapper">
  <div id="page">
<div id="header_line_top"></div>
<div id="header">
      <?php
      $a = new Area('Header Nav');
      $a->display($c);
      ?>
</div>
<div id="header_line_bottom"></div>
```

What just happened?

There are a few highlighted lines in the preceding code, which we modified in order to use our HTML code in concrete5:

◆ The first line makes sure you can't directly call our file to ensure that everything is running in the concrete5 context.

- The next two highlighted lines include our CSS files the proper concrete5 way. You can avoid the PHP function if you want but you'll get access to a nice concrete5 feature if you use `$this->getStyleSheet`, thanks to which you can easily change properties of your CSS file in a nice interface without touching a single line of code. There's more about it in this chapter in the *Customizable themes* section.

- `Loader::element` makes sure the concrete5 in-site editing toolbar is included. This is necessary to display the in-site editing toolbar, once you're logged in to your site.

- The last few highlighted lines define the place where blocks can be placed, an area. The string `Header Nav` is what the user is going to see while editing the page.

We've split a part of our HTML code into a new file named `header.php`. While this isn't mandatory, most themes follow this procedure and you probably should too, as long as you don't have any good reason not to.

Even if you just have one page layout, you never know what happens next and keeping your files clean and short makes it easier to read as well.

Let's create the next element, the footer!

Time for action – creating the concrete5 theme footer

Carry out the following steps:

1. In the `elements` directory, create a new file named `footer.php`.

2. From the original HTML file, copy everything starting at `footer_line_top` to the end of the file and insert it into the new file:

```php
<?php defined('C5_EXECUTE') or die(_("Access Denied.")); ?>
<div id="footer_line_top"></div>
<div id="footer"></div>
<div id="footer_line_bottom"></div>
</div>
</div>

<?php Loader::element('footer_required'); ?>
</body>
</html>
```

3. There are only two lines we have to insert. The first one is again, just a protection to disallow direct calls to our file. The second one is a placeholder for a snippet you can specify in the concrete5 dashboard. This is often used for a JavaScript statistics tracking code.

4. Save and close the file; there's nothing else to do in this file, as we're not having any dynamic content in this file.

What just happened?

We created another shared element which holds the code for our footer. There's not much code in it as we're trying to keep things simple and therefore, not putting any content in the footer.

In case you create some theme templates, you can use this footer for all of them, which makes sure that if you want a login link at the bottom you can do it once and it will appear on all page types and therefore all pages as well.

Time for action – creating a page template

Carry out the following steps:

1. Go back to the directory where you've created `description.txt` and create another file named `default.php`.

2. Insert the content `DIV` along with some PHP code:

```php
<?php
defined('C5_EXECUTE') or die(_("Access Denied."));
$this->inc('elements/header.php');
?>

<div id="content">
<?php
$b = new Area('Main');
$b->display($c);
?>
</div>

<?php $this->inc('elements/footer.php'); ?>
```

What just happened?

Just like we did in the header, there's a line at the top to avoid direct calls and a few more lines of code to insert another editable area named `Main`. As you can see, the creation of the last file was also quite easy. There isn't a lot left from the original HTML code. However, having a small `default.php` file is also quite helpful, as we have to extend this file in case we need more page templates.

Time for action – creating more page templates

Carry out the following steps:

1. concrete5 themes usually ship with a few default templates, one of them usually named `left_sidebar`. Let's create it by copying `default.php` in a new file named `left_sidebar.php`.

2. We're going to add two sub `DIV` elements to hold our left and main column:

```php
<?php
defined('C5_EXECUTE') or die(_("Access Denied."));
$this->inc('elements/header.php');
?>

<div id="content">
<div id="left-sidebar">
<?php
        $as = new Area('Sidebar');
        $as->display($c);
        ?>
</div>

<div id="main">
<?php
        $b = new Area('Main');
        $b->display($c);
        ?>
</div>

<div class="clear"></div>
</div>

<?php $this->inc('elements/footer.php'); ?>
```

3. As we've added new HTML elements, we also have to insert a few more CSS rules in `main.css`, as follows:

```css
#left-sidebar {
float: left;
width: 250px;
margin-right: 30px;
}
#main {
float: left;
```

```
width: 600px;
}
.clear {
clear: both;
}
```

4. Let's create another file named `right_sidebar.php`. Call the sidebar container `right-sidebar` and switch the two `DIV` elements. Some more CSS rules are necessary as well:

```
#right-sidebar {
float: left;
width: 250px;
margin-left: 30px;
}
```

What just happened?

We've created two more page templates for our site. If you edit a page, you can click on **Design** and select the left- and right-sidebar template to change the location of the sidebar.

While you probably remember the layouts you can create within each area by splitting an area into columns, it might have some advantages to create pages types as it is easier for the user to specify the layout when creating a new page. However, you're of course free to avoid additional templates by splitting an area into several columns. Up to whatever you like!

Pop quiz – what are page templates and page types?

What are page templates and page types used for?

- ◆ A page template is a physical file in your theme where you build your HTML structure to implement your site's layout(s)
- ◆ A page type always has its own page template
- ◆ A page type can have its own page templates but doesn't need to have one
- ◆ Unlike page templates, pages types can be used in the concrete5 interface as a logical element to filter and search for pages

Installing your theme

Once you've created all the files, you probably want to see how it looks on your site. As we've placed the files at the right place, we don't have to use `Add Functionality` in the dashboard, which is only necessary with blocks, packages, and themes wrapped in packages.

Time for action – installing theme

Carry out the following steps:

1. Go to the dashboard and click on **Pages and Themes**.

2. Your new theme should appear at the end of the installed themes; click on **Install**, as shown in the following screenshot:

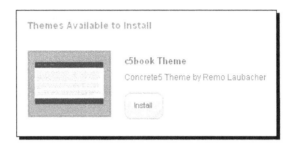

3. In the next screen, you'll see all the page templates you've created. Click on **Return to Themes** to get back to the previous screen.

4. You just installed your theme, but it isn't activated yet. Click on **Preview** if you want to look at it before activating it or just click on **Activate** to use it right away.

What just happened?

We've installed our new theme which has been converted from a static HTML page. A theme is nothing else but a bunch of files in a single directory, but it won't be available in concrete5 unless you follow the preceding steps.

PHP constants and functions

The following subchapter isn't one you have to go through step by step; it's rather a collection of small features that you can use to improve your concrete5 theme or block. The code snippets won't have any purpose in the upcoming chapters; you can implement them if you like, but you don't have to.

By default, concrete5 sets a bunch of constants that you can use when you create a theme but also a block or any other type of add-on. Most of them aren't really useful, they are needed by concrete5 within the core, but some are necessary and the rest give you an impression about a few internal aspects of concrete5. There are also lots of functions, some of them quite handy when you work within a theme template.

While the basic template we've created works well for most situations, there are several things you can do within a template and not only in the user interface. The code lines aren't real life examples; they just give you a hint about things you can do once you run into a problem.

Again, instead of publishing a complete list of constants you might need, we're going to look at a simple way to get a list which will always show you all constants, no matter what version of concrete5 you're using.

Time for action – getting a list of available constants

Carry out the following steps to get a list of available constants:

1. Open `default.php` from your theme in a text editor.

2. Look for the following PHP block:

```php
<?php
$b = new Area('Main');
$b->display($c);
?>
```

3. Before the closing PHP tags `?>`, insert a few more lines so it looks like the following:

```php
<?php
$b = new Area('Main');
$b->display($c);
echo '<xmp>';
print_r(get_defined_constants(true));
echo '</xmp>';
?>
```

4. Open a page of a type without a page template. Remember, we've created a template for the left- and right-sidebars. Pick full width for example, otherwise the inserted code won't be executed.

5. The output will contain a huge list of constants categorized by modules. At the end there's a category named `user`; these are the constants which are not coming from PHP itself but rather from concrete5. Look at them and you'll find a lot of constants related to directories and URLs. They might be useful one day.

What just happened?

Even if you've built software for a long time you'll still find methods, properties, and a lot more you haven't used before. You can try to remember all of them, but you'll probably have a hard time doing so. The preceding code can help you to get some information about the constants used in a PHP project.

Time for action – list all available functions

As with most classes, you often have to call a method to get a value and not directly access a property as the method might do some additional checks you'd lose if you accessed the property directly.

1. To get a list of all available methods without looking into the code, just add the following code where you'd like to get more information. Let's put it in `default.php` again like we did with the constants:

    ```php
    <?php
    $b = new Area('Main');
    $b->display($c);

    echo '<xmp>';
    $reflection = new ReflectionClass($this);
    print_r($reflection->getMethods());
    echo '</xmp>';
    ?>
    ```

2. This will print a long list where you can find all the available methods next to the property named `name`:

    ```
    Array
    (
        [0] =>ReflectionMethod Object
            (
                [name] =>getInstance
                [class] => View
            )

        [1] =>ReflectionMethod Object
            (
                [name] =>getThemeFromPath
                [class] => View
            )
    ```

What just happened?

The preceding *Time for action* section prints all available methods in the current context, helping you to get a first impression about the available methods. The last two *Time for actions* sections can be used in other PHP based projects.

You won't get a nice explanation about the constants or methods, but you'll still know if something is available, helping you to be sure that you're on the right track.

Time for action – checking for edit mode

There are situations where you have to know if the user is currently editing the page. For example, the in-site editing toolbar sometimes causes problems because it shifts down a few elements. If your layout has been built using absolutely positioned layers, you probably have to move down the layers a bit in case the toolbar is visible.

The current page object can be accessed by using the variable $c, which contains a method that returns true if the page is currently in the edit mode. The following code will output a short sentence, but only if the page is in the edit mode. You can put the following little bit of code in default.php again or any other template you like:

```php
<?php
if ($c->isEditMode()) {
echo 'You are editing this page at the moment!';
}

$b = new Area('Main');
$b->display($c);
?>
```

What just happened?

By calling the isEditMode method on the current page, which you can access by $c, you can check if the user is currently editing the page. This offers you some flexibility in case a layout or block causes problems in the edit mode. This simple check makes it easy to change, hide, or disable certain functions on your site if it's necessary.

Time for action – hiding content from anonymous visitors

Carry out the following steps:

1. We've already seen how we can hide a page or even a block from a user by using the concrete5 user interface in combination with the advanced permission mode.

2. Let's hide content by using some code. Put the following lines in `default.php`:

```php
<?php
$u = new User();
if ($u->isLoggedIn()) {
echo '<a href="/secret/">Secret key to world domination</a>';
}

$b = new Area('Main');
$b->display($c);
?>
```

What just happened?

The preceding two *Time for action* sections can both be used to change the content by adding some logic to the template.

While we've put both of them in a theme template, they are not only restricted to this location. You can use the command `new User` almost anywhere in concrete5. The method `isEditMode` also works at several places, theme templates, page list templates, or autonav templates.

Time for action – restricting numbers of blocks per area

By default, you can place as many blocks in an area as you want. However, there are situations where a restriction to a single block might have some advantages.

In an absolute positioned layout, it can happen that the `Add To Main` link overlaps with another area or you simply want to make sure that there's just a single image block in the header area.

1. Open the theme template where you'd like to add a restriction to the number of blocks. `default.php` does the job again.

2. Look for the PHP part where you specify the area and insert the highlighted line shown here:

```php
<?php
$b = new Area('Main');
$b->setBlockLimit(1);
$b->display($c);
?>
```

What just happened?

By simply adding one more line to our area, we made sure that only one block can be inserted. This nifty little method makes sure that the interface stays clean and consistent. If you've made a wrong decision, no worries—the line can be removed without any problems at any time.

Time for action – inserting block wrapper in area

While you can do a lot with the CSS layout feature in concrete5, it might be the case that you have to surround your block with some HTML code to style your site the way you want it to look like. There's a simple way to add some wrapping code around each block in an area, as follows:

1. Once more, open a theme template like `default.php` and look for the place where you create the area.

2. Replace the PHP block using the following snippet:

```php
<?php
$b = new Area('Main');
$b->setBlockWrapperStart('<div class="mainBlock">');
$b->setBlockWrapperEnd('</div>');
$b->display($c);
?>
```

What just happened?

The two lines of PHP code we've inserted in the preceding snippet simply surround each block in the Main area with a DIV element.

When you now create your CSS file, you can access them using `.mainBlock`. A few lines in your CSS file like the following will add a line at the bottom of each block:

```
.mainBlock {
border-top: 1px solid black;
}
```

Working with page attributes

concrete5 ships with a few default attributes on pages, users, and files. You can easily add new attributes to these objects to attach different kind of metadata to them. You can use attributes to create dynamic elements in your theme without creating your own block.

A few things you can do with the default attributes:

◆ Exclude a page from the navigation

◆ Specify metadata for search engines

◆ Exclude a page from the search index

These are just a few things you can do by default, without adding a new attribute. However, what can we do if we create our own attributes?

Imagine we'd like to have a different background picture on each page. We could create a block for this, but we can also use an attribute and a little modification to our theme.

Time for action – using attributes to set background picture

Carry out the following steps:

1. Go to the dashboard and click on **Pages and Themes** and then **Attributes**.

2. At the bottom, select **Image/File** and click on **Go**.

3. In the next screen, enter `background` for **Handle** and `Background Picture` in **Name**. The handle is what you'll need to access your attribute from code.

4. Click on **Add Attribute**.

5. Go to **Page Types**.

6. Click on **Edit** next to the first page type.

7. In the middle, check the checkbox next to **Background Picture**. This makes sure the attribute is displayed by default for each page of this type. You can add attributes to a page, even if this checkbox isn't checked, but it saves one click.

8. Click on **Update Page Type**.

9. Do the same for all page types where you'd like to use this attribute.

10. Go to the home page and enable the edit mode.

11. Click on **Properties** and select the last tab **Custom Attributes**. This is where you can find all the attributes on a page.

12. Use the file selector next to our new attribute to select a new background picture for the current page.

13. Click on **Save** and the selected picture will be assigned to our page.

What just happened?

We've created a new image attribute, which we're using to assign a background picture to a page of our choice.

This procedure works with every attribute, text, number, dates, and a few more. You can use them in the same way if you want to manage page specific metadata.

It's now possible to assign pictures to a page, but nothing happens with this data at the moment. We've got to add a few lines of code to display the new background picture.

Time for action – accessing attribute data from a template

Carry out the following steps:

1. Open `header.php` of your theme in your editor.

2. Remove the `<body>` tag; we're going to replace it with some code, which includes the background picture.

3. Insert the following code right where you've removed the `<body>` tag:

    ```php
    <?php
    $backgroundAttribute = $c->getAttribute('background');
    if ($backgroundAttribute) {
     $backgroundFile = $backgroundAttribute->getRelativePath();
     echo "<body style=\"background:url('{$backgroundFile}')\">";
    }
    else {
    echo "<body>";
    }
    ?>
    ```

4. Reload your page and you'll see the new background picture instead of the color gray.

What just happened?

We removed the static body tag and inserted some PHP code to fetch the attribute value. This works by using `$c->getAttribute`. `$c` is a global variable referring to the current page.

getAttribute is a method available on all collection objects like pages. This method works for all attributes but depending on the attribute type, you'll get a different object back. While a text attribute returns a discrete value, a complex attribute type such as an address or an image will return an object with several properties. How do you know what to do with the attribute value? Use the following code to find all the properties; insert it right after <body> in the template of your theme:

```php
<?php
$attr = $c->getAttribute('background');
echo '<xmp>';
print_r($attr);
echo '</xmp>';
?>
```

This will print something like the following:

```
File Object
(
    [error] =>
    [fID] => 11
    [fDateAdded] => 2010-09-03 16:05:20
    [uID] => 1
    [fslID] => 0
    [fOverrideSetPermissions] => 0
    [fPassword] =>
    [fvID] => 1
)
```

What does this tell you? First and most important, the PHP object has been instantiated from the class File. You can also see a few properties which might give you a first impression about the data accessible from the object. However, in this case, it won't reveal a lot though.

You'll need some knowledge of object oriented programming, but once you know that the attribute class is a File, you can quickly open concrete/models/file.php and have a look at all the available methods. It might be a bit confusing if you look at this file for the first time, but if you have the basic knowledge, take the time and you'll soon realize that the concrete5 framework is easier than you probably think right now.

You won't find our method getRelativePath in the File class, as the call will be forwarded to a PHP method named __call, which will try to look for the method in the latest approved file version class which you can find in file_version.php. There you'll find most methods you'll need when working with files like getRelativePath, getSize, getAuthorName, and more. Don't worry if you're confused by this, it's not a must to understand these procedures, but it will definitely help you at some point, especially if you plan to build your own blocks and packages.

Pop quiz – what are attributes?

What are attributes in concrete5?

- ◆ Attributes are settings you can apply to the HTML code of your concrete5 theme.
- ◆ Attributes are flexible add-ons you can assign to all objects in concrete5 like pages, page types, groups, maintenance jobs, and so on.
- ◆ Attributes can have different types like numbers, checkboxes, and files. You can create and assign them to users, pages, and files.
- ◆ concrete5 uses attributes to classify all pages of a site making it easier to keep an overview of them.

Block in templates

Putting blocks in areas is a rather simple task, but if your users aren't experienced computer users, it might be even too easy. What if they accidentally delete or modify the autonav, the navigation block? It would break the site very quickly.

You can enable the advanced permission mode, which allows you to specify permission on blocks and areas. However, enabling this mode can give you too much power and makes managing the site more complicated. While this shouldn't be a problem once you're more familiar with concrete5, there's another way you might want to check out—put block in your templates!

Time for action – replacing header area with template block

Carry out the following steps:

1. Open `elements/header.php` from your theme in your text editor.

2. Look for the following highlighted lines and remove all of them:

```
<div id="wrapper">
<div id="page">
<div id="header_line_top"></div>
<div id="header">
<?php
$a = new Area('Header Nav');
$a->display($c);
?>
</div>
```

3. Next, insert the following PHP code instead:

```php
<?php
$autonav = BlockType::getByHandle('autonav');
$autonav->controller->orderBy = 'display_asc';
$autonav->controller->displayPages = 'top';
$autonav->render('templates/header_menu');
?>
```

4. Save the file and reload your page. The header navigation is still there, but if you switch into edit mode, there's nothing you can edit in the header navigation.

What just happened?

By replacing the area with the small code above, we've put the autonav block directly into the template disallowing any modification in the user interface.

We've set a few properties to specify the intended autonav behavior and called render with the argument `templates/header_menu`. This makes sure we're using the header menu template which you can find in `concrete/blocks/autonav/templates`. Please note, there's no `.php` extension when calling the render method.

If you want to use the default template of a block, just specify `view`:

```php
$autonav->render('view');
```

Putting blocks in a template using this procedure works for almost any block, but how do you know what kind of properties they have?

Time for action – finding autonav block properties

There are several tools doing a similar job, but Firefox in combination with Firebug has proven to be a solid choice. Install Firefox if you haven't done that already.

1. Navigate to `http://getfirebug.com/` and click on **Install Firebug For Firefox**.

2. After the installation procedure has succeeded, log in to your concrete5 test site `http://localhost/login/`.

3. Navigate to the home page and switch to the edit mode. Click on **Add to Main** and **Add Block**.

4. Pick the block you want to find the properties for. Autonav is a good choice as it has a few properties you might not find very intuitive.

5.   When the block edit dialog is visible, right click on the first drop-down list, as shown in the following screenshot:

6.   The Firebug add-on has added a new menu item **Inspect Element** (as shown in the preceding screenshot) click on it and Firebug will be displayed.

7.   The focus should be set on the `select` element named `orderBy`. Expand it by clicking on the small plus sign in front of it, as shown in the following screenshot:

```
<strong> Pages Should Appear </strong>
<br>
<select name="orderBy">
    <option value="display_asc"> in their sitemap
    order. </option>
    <option value="chrono_desc"> with the most recent
    first. </option>
    <option value="chrono_asc"> with the earliest
    first. </option>
    <option value="alpha_asc"> in alphabetical order.
    </option>
    <option value="alpha_desc"> in reverse alphabetical
    order. </option>
    <option value="display_desc"> in reverse sitemap
    order. </option>
</select>
```

8.   This little Firebug screen tells you a lot: First, you can see the name of the property, `orderBy`. Each option element has a value like `display_asc`, which is what you have to use in the code along with the explanation you can also see in the form.

What just happened?

Using Firebug, we discovered where we can quickly find all the block properties. concrete5 block edit dialogs work like a common HTML form and therefore, use tags like `input` and `select` to update the block properties.

While this might be an uncommon kind of documentation, it will work with blocks which have been released a minute ago, even if the developer didn't take the time to write the documentation.

In the case of autonav, a complete example with all available properties would look like the following:

```
$autonav = BlockType::getByHandle('autonav');
$autonav->controller->orderBy = 'display_asc';
$autonav->controller->displayUnavailablePages = 1;
$autonav->controller->displayPages = 'top';
$autonav->controller->displaySubPages = 'relevant';
$autonav->controller->displaySubPageLevels = 'enough_plus1';
$autonav->render('view');
```

Time for action – specifying block template in area

Sometimes you might want to set a default block template for an area. This might happen if the default template doesn't work at all and the customer would have to select a custom template for each block he adds. Let's save his time and specify a block template in our template:

1. Open a theme template like `default.php`

2. Look for the PHP block which defines an area and insert the highlighted line from the following snippet:

```
<?php
$b = new Area('Main');
$b->setCustomTemplate('autonav', 'templates/header_menu');
$b->display($c);
?>
```

What just happened?

The single line of code that we've added to our theme templates makes sure that for every autonav block where no template has manually been specified in the user interface, the `header_menu` template is used.

While setting `header_menu` for all autonav blocks is probably a bit useless, you'll learn how to build your own block templates in the next chapter. Once you've created your own templates, it's just a matter of time until you realize that overriding the default block template can be quite handy.

Applying theme to single page

There are a few pages in concrete5 you don't have to create on your own. They exist whether you like it or not but luckily the chances are good you'll like them.

Assume you're using the existing login page you can find at `http://localhost/login/` to grant some visitors access to the VIP section on your page. This works out of the box but it doesn't look like it should; it still has the classic concrete5 look and doesn't look like our site at all.

To apply the look of our site, we have to do two things. Create a special file in our theme to handle these pages and activate the theme for these pages. The next two *Time for action* sections are going to do these steps.

What's a single page?

A single page is a page which is likely to exist just once in your site. This is usually due to a certain complexity or layout like the dashboard pages. A second dashboard setting page is quite useless, which is why it has been built using a single page.

For those familiar with other MVC frameworks, single pages are usually called **views** or **layouts**.

Time for action – creating single page layout

Carry out the following steps:

1. Create a file named `view.php` in your theme.

2. Put the following code in it:

```php
<?php
defined('C5_EXECUTE') or die(_("Access Denied."));
$this->inc('elements/header.php');
?>

<div id="content">
<?php
```

```
echo $innerContent;
?>
</div>


<?php $this->inc('elements/footer.php'); ?>
```

What just happened?

We've created another file in our theme which looks a lot like `default.php`. However, there's one major difference, `view.php` must always output the variable `$innerContent`. The content of single pages is generated by program code and saved in `$innerContent`.

Some controllers use more variables which you'll have to process as well in order to replace the concrete5 core layout. The login page for example has another variable in order to make sure errors are printed too.

Time for action – adding variables to handle login errors

Carry out the following steps:

1. Before you put any code in `view.php`, open `concrete\themes\core\concrete.php` and have a look at the content of the file. Right before `$innerContent` is printed there are a few lines about printing any existing errors. This is what we're going to need in our `view.php` too. Copy and insert it in the new file, and it should look like the following:

```php
<?php
defined('C5_EXECUTE') or die( _("Access Denied."));
$this->inc('elements/header.php');
?>


<div id="content">

<?php  if (isset($error) && $error != '') { ?>
<?php
if ($error instanceof Exception) {
$_error[] = $error->getMessage();
} else if ($error instanceofValidationErrorHelper) {
$_error = $error->getList();
} else if (is_array($error)) {
$_error = $error;
} else if (is_string($error)) {
$_error[] = $error;
}
```

```
?>
<ul class="ccm-error">
<?php foreach($_error as $e) { ?><li><?php echo $e?>
  </li><?php  } ?>
</ul>
<?php
} ?>
```

```
<?php
echo $innerContent;
?>
</div>
```

```
<?php $this->inc('elements/footer.php'); ?>
```

2. Now that we handle errors as well; we can use our `view.php` to style the login page. Open `config/site_theme_paths.php` in your editor.

3. There are already a few examples we can use as a template, or simply remove everything and insert the following lines instead:

```
<?php
defined('C5_EXECUTE') or die(_("Access Denied."));
$v = View::getInstance();
$v->setThemeByPath('/login', "c5book");
```

4. Save the file and log out of concrete5 and go to `http://localhost/login/`.

What just happened?

We've added `view.php` to our theme which can be used to apply a theme layout to single pages. The login page has now been embedded into our page with a small modification to `config/site_theme_paths.php`.

We're going to create our own single pages later in this book as well, but if you just want to style existing single pages, this is everything you'll need.

Pop quiz – what's a single page?

1. A page like the one available at `http://localhost/login/` is called single page in concrete5. What are they?

    a. Single pages are regular pages without a different to a page.

    b. They are used for pages with a unique functionality not needed in other places of the site.

    c. Single pages are built using custom code following the MVC pattern.

    d. Dashboard pages, as well as extensions to the dashboard by add-ons are built using single pages.

2. In which situation would you consider using a single page? Please note that it's not always a must to use a single page, but rather a recommendation.

    a. A configuration page part of an add-on visible in the dashboard.

    b. As a contact form to let your website visitors send you a message though a form.

    c. A custom 404 page to handle requests to pages not available anymore.

    d. The member profile of your community with lots of custom functionality.

Creating a customizable theme

Creating a concrete5 theme does require some programming skills; it's a tool for programmers and not just designers and end-users after all. However, there's a nice way to allow end users to change some colors in a theme without any programming skill.

There's a simple way to create customizable CSS styles in almost no time. This feature allows you to change colors and fonts and insert custom CSS rules using the concrete5 interface without touching any files at all.

Time for action – a creating customizable theme

Carry out the following steps:

1. Open `main.css` from your theme.

2. There are several rules we have to replace; search for all of them and replace it with the new code.

3. Look for `body` and replace it using the following code:

```
body {
    /* customize_background */ background-color: #989898;
    /* customize_background */
    height: 100%;
}
```

4. Search for `#header_line_bottom` and replace it with these lines:

```
#header_line_bottom {
    /* customize_header_line */ background-color: #e64116;
    /* customize_header_line */
    height: 3px;
}
```

5. Search for `#footer_line_top` and replace it with the following lines:

```
#footer_line_top {
    /* customize_footer_line */ background-color: #e64116;
    /* customize_footer_line */
    height: 3px;
}
```

6. At the end of the file, insert the following line:

```
/* customize_miscellaneous */ /* customize_miscellaneous */
```

What just happened?

We've added some comments to our CSS file; they don't generate any errors if you validate the file but concrete5 parses them and generates an interface on top of it where you can change the values surrounded by these comments.

After you've saved the modified CSS file, you can navigate to **Pages and Themes** and click on **Customize** next to the active theme. All the comments are transferred into a simple interface where you can change the values by clicking on the icon on the left of each property. Change them and you'll immediately see a preview of how the page is going to look with the new values. If you're satisfied with your choice, click on **Save** and your site will be going green in no time, as shown in the following screenshot:

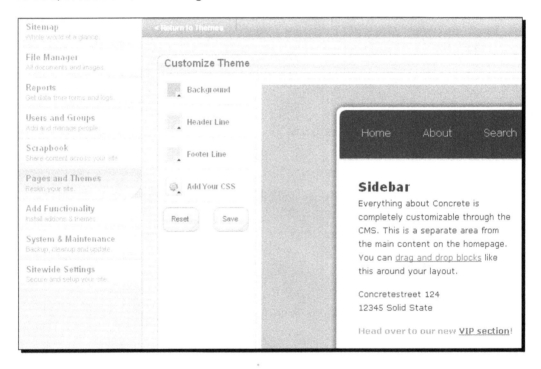

It often happens that a new theme ignores the custom values. This is usually due to a problem in the way the CSS file is included. If it has been directly linked using a relative path, concrete5 won't be able to replace the values. Make sure you use the following code to include your CSS file in case you want to use customizable style sheets:

```
<link rel="stylesheet" media="screen" type="text/css" href="<?php echo
$this->getStyleSheet('main.css')?>" />
```

Summary

In this chapter, we've looked at the process to transform a static HTML site into a concrete5 theme by adding a few PHP calls in our files. We've split our theme into three parts, a header, the actual content file, and a footer to make it easier to create different page templates to allow a quick change of the page structure.

After we finished our theme, we installed it, and had a look at different functions you might be able to use in case you want to get a little bit more out of concrete5.

Afterwards, we created a new page attribute where we can assign a page specific background picture. The attribute example was rather simple, but once you've got into it, you should be able to come up with a lot of different applications for attributes.

Next, we added a navigation block right into our template to avoid the need to use page defaults or manually add the navigation on each page. This also made it impossible for the end user to accidentally remove or modify the navigation, a part of the site which is quite likely not to change every day.

We've also looked at a way to assign our page theme to existing single pages such as the login page. This allows us to use built in concrete5 functionality for a community without having to write lots of code.

If you followed each step of this chapter, you should have created a bunch of files for your concrete5 site. For those who were in a rush or accidentally skipped a step, you can download the complete theme in the `4286_05_c5book_theme.zip` folder on the Packt website

Extract the file in `/themes` and you can install it when you go to **Pages and Themes** in the dashboard of your site.

6
Customizing Block Layout

In the previous chapter we looked at themes to customize the site's layout. While this has probably been the more important part, concrete5 does not limit you to page layout customization. You can also adapt every block layout to suit your needs, without touching its actual logic, the inner working of it.

You can use PHP logic as well as JavaScript and CSS to change the output of a block with this feature.

Custom templates to modify block layout

In *Chapter 4* we had a first quick look at the structure of a block. We're going to take a deeper look at two elements of that structure:

- ◆ `view.php`: We're going to refer to it as the **default block template**. It's the file responsible for the output of the block.

- ◆ `templates`: This directory contains more (optional) block templates. Some blocks already come with several templates, and some only with the default block template.

What does this mean in more detail?

- ◆ A core custom template can be found in `/concrete/blocks/<block-name>/templates`. Custom templates are optional though, you won't find a lot of templates by default.

- ◆ A custom template could also be placed in `/blocks/<block-name>/templates`. What's the difference to the location mentioned above? You should avoid making any modification to a file in the `concrete` directory. This is why it's possible to override templates by using the same path without concrete at the beginning, which will make it possible to update concrete5 without losing your modifications.

♦ If there's no custom template, the block will either use `view.php` from this location `/concrete/blocks/<block-name>` or `/blocks/<block-name>`. Again, the latter path would be chosen if `view.php` existed in both locations.

When you click on a block you've added, there's a menu item called **Custom Template**:

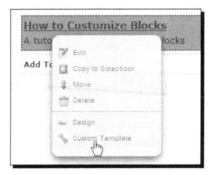

After you've clicked on it, a small dialog appears with a list of available templates:

If you pick **(None selected)** the block will use the default block template `view.php`. As of now, only the `autonav` and `page_list` blocks come with additional templates.

Thumbnails in a page list

Earlier in this book, we added a page list in the news page to display all child pages. If that's not the case anymore, go to the **News** page and add a page list block and select **beneath this page** to display the child pages.

This block makes it easy to create a list of pages—whether we're using it to display news, an archive, or products. There's a title and a description and that's basically it.

Like most news pages, we're going to use a thumbnail to give the visitor a better impression of the article.

Time for action – adding thumbnails to a page list

You can add thumbnails to your page list by following these steps:

1. In the dashboard, go to **Pages and Themes** and then **Attributes**. Choose **Image/File** and click on **Go** to add the new attribute.

2. Enter `thumbnail` in **Handle** and `Thumbnail` for **Name**.

3. Go to the sitemap and open the properties for the child page of **News**:

4. Activate the **Custom Attribute** register.

5. Select our new attribute **Thumbnail** from the drop down list.

6. Scroll down and select a picture you'd like to use for this page.

7. Hit **Save** to confirm the modification to the page.

8. We've entered all the data, so let's create the new template. Copy the file `concrete\blocks\page_list\view.php` to a new file at the location `blocks\page_list\templates\news.php`. You might have to create the directories `page_list` and `templates` within each other.

9. Open the new file and look for the code printed below. It's the main loop which goes through an array of pages supplied by the page list controller. This loop is what we have to modify to output the picture associated with the page:

```php
<?php
for ($i = 0; $i < count($cArray); $i++ ) {
    $cobj = $cArray[$i];
    $title = $cobj->getCollectionName(); ?>
```

```
<h3 class="ccm-page-list-title"><a href="<?php echo $nh->getLinkTo
Collection($cobj)?>"><?php echo $title?></a></h3>
<div class="ccm-page-list-description">
    <?php
    if(!$controller->truncateSummaries){
        echo $cobj->getCollectionDescription();
    }else{
      echo $textHelper->shorten($cobj->getCollectionDescription(),
        $controller->truncateChars);
    }
    ?>
</div>
```

10. In the previous chapter we've used $c in a theme template to access our page. In the page list, we've got several pages in a loop. With each iteration, $cobj gets updated with the next page in the list. While the variable has a different name, it still refers to the same class, which means that all methods we've used before work on $cobj as well.

We're going to use getAttribute again to get our thumbnail and print it before the description:

```
<?php
for ($i = 0; $i < count($cArray); $i++ ) {
    $cobj = $cArray[$i];
    $title = $cobj->getCollectionName(); ?>

<h3 class="ccm-page-list-title"><a href="<?php echo $nh->getLinkTo
Collection($cobj)?>"><?php echo $title?></a></h3>
<?php
$thumbnail = $cobj->getAttribute('thumbnail');
if ($thumbnail) { ?>
    <div class="ccm-page-list-thumbnail"><img src="<?php echo
$thumbnail->getRelativePath() ?>" alt=""/></div>
<?php } ?>
<div class="ccm-page-list-description">
    <?php
    if(!$controller->truncateSummaries){
      echo $cobj->getCollectionDescription();
    }else{
      echo $textHelper->shorten($cobj->getCollectionDescription(),
        $controller->truncateChars);
    }
    ?>
</div>
```

11. Once you've saved your new template `news.php`, go back to the news page and activate the edit mode.

12. Click on the page list block and select **Set Custom Template**. In the dialog, pick our template and click on **Update**.

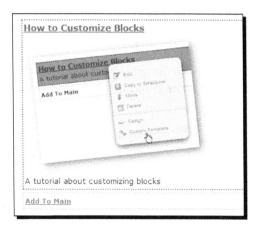

What just happened?

We made a copy of the default page list template and created a new one which prints the picture selected in the `thumbnail` attribute.

By making a copy of `view.php` outside of the `concrete` directory, we made sure that a future update to a newer concrete5 version doesn't affect our template.

You may have noticed this; the template name in the user interface started with a capital letter and didn't have a PHP extension at the end. concrete5 tries to keep the user interface as easy as possible and hides some of the cryptic programmer stuff. There's a little convention in the template name:

- Template names in the interface start with a capital letter
- There's no PHP at the end
- The letter after an underscore is uppercase

This means that the file name `packt_publishing.php` would be displayed as `Packt Publishing`.

While the template we've created should work quite well, you might get a huge picture in the page list because we output the image with the same dimensions as you've uploaded it. Wouldn't it be nice if concrete5 could restrict the maximum dimensions of the thumbnail?

Time for action – restricting thumbnail dimension

You can make concrete5 restrict the maximum thumbnail dimensions by taking the following steps:

1. concrete5 generates system thumbnails for every graphic file. There are two levels we can use by default: level 1 with a maximum dimension of 60 x 60 pixels and level 2 with a maximum dimension of 250 x 250 pixels.

2. The file object returned by `getAttribute` has a method called `getThumbnail` which we can use to access the thumbnail. After the modification, the template should look like this:

```php
<?php
for ($i = 0; $i < count($cArray); $i++ ) {
    $cobj = $cArray[$i];
    $title = $cobj->getCollectionName(); ?>

<h3 class="ccm-page-list-title"><a href="<?php echo $nh->getLinkTo
Collection($cobj)?>"><?php echo $title?></a></h3>
<?php
$thumbnail = $cobj->getAttribute('thumbnail');
if ($thumbnail) {
    echo '<div class="ccm-page-list-thumbnail">';
    echo $thumbnail->getThumbnail(2);
    echo '</div>';
} ?>
<div class="ccm-page-list-description">
    <?php
    if(!$controller->truncateSummaries){
        echo $cobj->getCollectionDescription();
    }else{
        echo $textHelper->shorten($cobj->getCollectionDescription(
),$controller->truncateChars);
    }
    ?>
</div>
```

What just happened?

By using the `getThumbnail` method, which is part of the file version object, we replaced the original picture with the default thumbnail that concrete5 automatically generates. The new code makes sure you're never going to see a picture bigger than 250 x 250 pixels, even if someone uploaded a picture straight from the latest digital camera model.

Time for action – restricting thumbnails to a custom dimension

Sometimes you might have to specify an exact dimension to suit your needs. concrete5 has several helper classes, one called image which offers several functions, including a function which generates and caches a thumbnail.

```php
<?php
$imageHelper = Loader::helper("image");
for ($i = 0; $i < count($cArray); $i++ ) {
    $cobj = $cArray[$i];
    $title = $cobj->getCollectionName(); ?>


<h3 class="ccm-page-list-title"><a href="<?php echo $nh->getLinkToColl
ection($cobj)?>"><?php echo $title?></a></h3>
<?php
$thumbnail = $cobj->getAttribute('thumbnail');
if ($thumbnail) {
    $thumbnailObj = $imageHelper->getThumbnail($thumbnail,200,200);
    echo '<div class="ccm-page-list-thumbnail">';
    echo "<img src=\"{$thumbnailObj->src}\" alt=\"\" width=\
"{$thumbnailObj->width}\" height=\"{$thumbnailObj->height}\"/>";
    echo '</div>';
} ?>
<div class="ccm-page-list-description">
    <?php
    if(!$controller->truncateSummaries){
        echo $cobj->getCollectionDescription();
    }else{
        echo $textHelper->shorten($cobj->getCollectionDescription(),
            $controller->truncateChars);
    }
    ?>
</div>
```

What just happened?

We extended the first template to assure the thumbnails don't exceed a certain dimension. The image we used in the last example, works not only within `templates`, but also in a controller, theme template, or any other file which is part of the concrete5 framework.

The image helper function we used, made sure that the thumbnail was cached in order to avoid unnecessary CPU time for further page views.

Having some knowledge about methods of classes available in concrete5 usually helps you a lot, no matter what kind of add-on you're working on. While it might be a bit overwhelming at the beginning, at least try to remember the methods mentioned in this book. Once you get more used to the concrete5 framework you'll quickly be able to learn new methods.

Have a go hero – improving thumbnail page list

Page types can be assigned attributes which will be displayed automatically, without selecting them in the drop down list. Try to create a new page type called News to make it easier and quicker to add a new News page.

The page list has a thumbnail but still looks rather simple and not very stylish. Since we've assigned our new element a CSS class called `ccm-page-list-thumbnail` you can easily access the element and change its layout. Try to use it in your theme to improve the layout. Make the thumbnail appear on the left of the description, add a line at the end of each list, and make other such improvements.

Have a go hero – explore concrete5 helpers

We did take a quick look at the image helper to generate a thumbnail, but concrete5 helpers not only help you to generate thumbnails but also e-mails, HTML forms, JSON strings, and a lot more.

You can find them by opening the directory `concrete\helpers`. You'll need a few of them later in this book, but we can't cover all of them.

Template folder

In the previous example, we created a single file used as a custom template. Instead of having just a single file, a template can also be a folder containing several files. This allows you to put CSS and JavaScript files and your template in a single directory. It also makes sure that CSS and JavaScript files are properly included in the header of your page.

Time for action – creating a template folder

Follow these steps to create a folder for your templates:

1. Create a new folder in `blocks\page_list\templates` called `news_2`.

2. Copy the previously created `news.php` file into this directory and rename it `view.php`.

3. Create a new file called `view.css` with the following content:

```
.ccm-page-list {
    border-bottom: 1px solid gray;
    padding-bottom: 20px;
    margin-bottom: 20px;
}
.ccm-page-list a {
    color: #262626;
}
```

What just happened?

We created a folder instead of a single file for our template. While `view.php` is mandatory, there are lots of optional files you can use. Within a template in the templates folder, the following are the files included by concrete5 in the header:

- `view.js`
- `view.css`
- `js/<anything>.js`
- `css/<anything>.css`

Whether you put the CSS rules in your theme or template using `view.css` or the `css` folder has to be decided for each situation. There's not a single correct answer. But think about whether you would like to reuse the template for other projects. If a template doesn't work at all without the CSS rules, it might be better to put them in the template as this makes it possible to copy and paste a single folder into a new project.

1. Let's say you created a template for the content block found at the following location: `blocks\content\templates\my_template`. How could you include the CSS and JavaScript files without touching any line of code in the core?

    a. All files with the extension `.js` located in the directory called `js`.

    b. All files with the extension `.css` or `.js`.

    c. All files with the extension `.css` located in the directory called `css`.

    d. Files in the root of the template directory called `view.css` or `view.js`.

Picture pop-ups in content block

concrete5 contains a bunch of add-ons by default and a lot more can be downloaded or bought at the marketplace. While you definitely find a lot of really nice add-ons, sometimes you can easily rebuild things with just a few small tricks.

Let's assume you've got a blog style page where you have some pictures in the text. It would be nice if you could click on them like a gallery, wouldn't it?

jQuery is the preferred JavaScript library of concrete5 and is included by default. It usually makes sense to use jQuery based libraries to avoid any conflicts between JavaScript libraries. Using jQuery, MooTools, and YUI at the same time works, but you have to make some modifications which can be time consuming and annoying. To keep this easy, we're going to use jQuery lightbox written by Leandro Vieira which you can download at:

`http://leandrovieira.com/projects/jquery/lightbox/.`

To build a lightbox gallery follow these steps:

1. Create the following directory: `blocks/content/templates/lightbox`.

2. Copy `concrete/blocks/content/view.php` into the new directory, keep the filename `view.php`.

3. From the downloaded jQuery ZIP file, extract the folders `images`, `css`, and `js` but make sure there's only `jquery.lightbox-0.5.min.js` in it—you have to remove all the other JavaScript files.

4. Add another file called `view.js` in the same directory as `view.php`. We need it to initialize the lightbox script. Its content has to look like this:

```
$(document).ready(function() {
    $("a.lightbox").lightBox({
        imageBtnPrev: CCM_REL + "/blocks/content/templates/lightbox/
images/lightbox-btn-prev.gif",
        imageBtnNext: CCM_REL + "/blocks/content/templates/lightbox/
images/lightbox-btn-next.gif",
        imageLoading: CCM_REL + "/blocks/content/templates/lightbox/
images/lightbox-ico-loading.gif",
        imageBtnClose: CCM_REL + "/blocks/content/templates/
lightbox/images/lightbox-btn-close.gif",
        imageBlank: CCM_REL + "/blocks/content/templates/lightbox/
images/lightbox-blank.gif"
    });
});
```

5. Go to the page where you'd like to insert a lightbox gallery and add a new content block.

6. Enter a text like `Skyline` and select it.

7. Click on **Add File** in the toolbar on top of the text editor. Select the picture you want to see when clicking on the link.

8. Update the content block and you should see a link called `Skyline` in it.

9. Click on the block and click on **Custom Template**. Select our template called **Lightbox**.

10. Exit the edit mode and publish the changes immediately.

11. Click on the link and you'll see the well-known lightbox effect in your concrete5 site for free.

What just happened?

We created another block template along with several folders and files to include the jQuery lightbox files. The only file we had to create was `view.js`, where we initialized the jQuery plugin, everything else was created by copy and paste action. If you're used to work with blocks and templates, this process takes very little time.

concrete5 uses jQuery as well - it is included by default - which makes it tricky to use other libraries such as MooTools or YUI. But luckily, you should be able to find more than enough jQuery libraries you can use for your page.

Have a go hero – creating another JavaScript gallery

While lightbox seems to be an obvious choice for a picture gallery nowadays, there are a lot more other galleries. You'll find lots of examples when you search for **jquery galleries** on Google.

Look for one you like and try to convert it into a concrete5 template. At the end of the chapter you can find another gallery template based on a script called `AD Gallery`.

Gravatar picture in guestbook

Gravatar is a widely used service to include a thumbnail of a person. It's a feature often used in blogs to display a face next to a comment. Internet users upload their picture at `http://en.gravatar.com/` and assign it to their e-mail address.

The application can then generate an md5 hash by using this e-mail address and can display an image of them, without exposing the actual mail address.

This procedure works with PHP like it does with any language where you can generate an md5 hash:

```
$gravatarHash = md5(strtolower(trim('your.mail@address.com')));
echo "<img src=\"http://www.gravatar.com/avatar/{$gravatarHash}\" />";
```

Let's add that feature to the guestbook block.

Time for action – adding a Gravatar picture to the guestbook

Follow these steps to easily add a Gravatar to the guestbook:

1. You will need to create the directory folder within `blocks`, `guestbook`, `templates` and copy the file from `concrete\blocks\guestbook\view.php` into the `templates` directory. After you've copied it, rename it to `gravatar.php` to make it clear what the templates are going to be used for.

2. The default block template contains quite a lot of code as it contains some functions to manage the comments. We won't have to bother with it, but we have to find our way around it. There are only a few lines we have to insert. Open `gravatar.php` and search for the following loop; it's not the whole content of the file! Insert the highlighted lines in your file:

```php
foreach($posts as $p) { ?>
  <?php  if($p['approved'] || $bp->canWrite()) { ?>
    <div class="guestBook-entry">
      <?php  if($bp->canWrite()) { ?>
        <div class="guestBook-manage-links">
          <a href="<?php echo $this->action('loadEntry')."&entryID
=".$p['entryID'];?>#guestBookForm"><?php echo t('Edit')?></a> |
          <a href="<?php echo $this->action('removeEntry')."&entry
ID=".$p['entryID'];?>" onclick="return confirm('<?php echo t("Are
you sure you would like to remove this comment?")?>');"><?php echo
t('Remove')?></a> |
            <?php  if($p['approved']) { ?>
              <a href="<?php echo $this->action('unApproveEntry').
"&entryID=".$p['entryID'];?>"><?php echo t('Un-Approve')?></a>
            <?php  } else { ?>
                <a href="<?php echo $this->action('approveEntr
y')."&entryID=".$p['entryID'];?>"><?php echo t('Approve')?></a>
            <?php  } ?>
        </div>
      <?php  } ?>
      <div class="contentByLine">

        <?php $gravatarHash = md5(strtolower(trim($p['user_
email'])));
        echo "<img style=\"float:left;margin-right: 10px;\"
src=\"http://www.gravatar.com/avatar/{$gravatarHash}\"
alt=\"\"/>";
            ?>

      <?php echo t('Posted by')?>
        <span class="userName">
          <?php

          if( intval($p['uID']) ){
            $ui = UserInfo::getByID(intval($p['uID']));
            if (is_object($ui)) {
              echo $ui->getUserName();
              }
            }else echo $p['user_name'];
          ?>
        </span>
        <?php echo t('on')?>
```

```
            <span class="contentDate">
              <?php echo date($dateFormat,strtotime($p['entryDate']
)) ;?>
            </span>
          </div>
          <?php echo nl2br($p['commentText'])?>

      <div style="clear:both"></div>
    </div>
  <?php } ?>
<?php }
```

3. Save the file and go back to your site and navigate to a page where you'd like the new guestbook to appear.

4. In the edit mode, add a new guestbook block to your page.

5. When added, click on it again and select **Custom Template** and find our new **Gravatar** template in the list.

6. Post a new comment and check what happens.

What just happened?

The new template we created adds a Gravatar thumbnail to the guestbook by extending the default block template with a few lines of additional code. If a person hasn't uploaded a picture, you'll see the default Gravatar picture, but the script still works.

Avoiding duplicate code in a custom template

You might have wondered why we always have to copy the whole template file in order to modify just a single line. While copying the file is okay, it makes sure the changes don't get lost when you update to a newer version of concrete5; there's an option to include an existing template in a new one.

This works nicely if you just want to wrap an existing template. Let's assume you want to add some CSS rules to a content block. You'll quickly realize that there's no wrapping DIV in it, which makes it hard to apply styles for the content block. You can override any paragraph but if that's not what you want to do you have to create a new template and add a surrounding DIV element.

Time for action – including an existing template

You can include an existing template on your concrete5 site by taking the following steps:

1. Create a new file at the following location:

   ```
   blocks/content/templates/wrapper.php.
   ```

2. Enter the following code in the new file:

   ```php
   <div class="content-wrapper">
   <?php
   $bvt = new BlockViewTemplate($b);
   $bvt->setBlockCustomTemplate(false);

   include($bvt->getTemplate());
   ?>
   </div>
   ```

3. Save the file and go back to your concrete5 site.

4. Add a new content block and click on it after you've hit **Update** and select **Custom Template**.

5. Select **Wrapper** and update again.

6. When you look at the HTML code generated by concrete5 you'll find an additional DIV with a class called content-wrapper.

7. You can use this class in your CSS file called main.css. Add a rule like this to change the background color:

   ```css
   .content-wrapper {
       background-color: silver;
   }
   ```

What just happened?

We created a new template which basically includes the existing content block default block template. There's just an additional HTML tag we've added to make it easier to access the content block output by CSS rules.

How did this work? We used the global variable `$b`, which contains the block view instance of the block for which we're creating a template.

We call `setBlockCustomTemplate` with `false` as its parameter to avoid rendering the custom template (our file). It temporarily disables the custom template and allows us to get the filename of the default block template by calling `getTemplate`. We include it and we're done.

This procedure is especially useful if you just want to add code to the beginning or end of an existing template. You can then be sure that once the default block template gets updated, it will be included in your own custom template.

You'll find a more useful example in the next section!

Auto-hide news page list

The page list has come in handy a few times already and now we have even more features to add. Let's assume your site has lots of visitors frequently looking for the top news on your site. Putting them on the landing page might work but search engines will quite likely forward your visitors to all kinds of sub-pages you created.

What could we do if we wanted to offer an easy access to our top news pages on every page? You could add a standard page list everywhere but that would take up space for which you probably have a better use. Couldn't we just add a **News** button which shows the list when the visitor hovers over the button? Not out of the box but you're just a few steps away from it!

Time for action – creating an auto-hide page list

Follow these steps to create an auto-hide page list:

1. Create a new directory structure for our template:

   `blocks/page_list/templates/auto_hide`.

2. Within that directory, create a new `view.php` file. We don't have to copy the original default block template as we're only going to surround the existing template with a few elements as shown in the previous section.

```
<div class="fixed-page-list<?php global $c; if ($c->isEditMode())
{ echo '-edit'; } ?>">
  <div class="fixed-page-list-content">
    <?php
    $bvt = new BlockViewTemplate($b);
    $bvt->setBlockCustomTemplate(false);

    include($bvt->getTemplate());
    ?>
  </div>
  <div class="fixed-page-list-button">
    News
  </div>
</div>
```

3. Create another file called `view.css`. Our **News** button is going to be attached to the left border of the browser window. To do this, we have to add some CSS rules, as follows:

```
.fixed-page-list {
  width:300px;
  height:300px;
  float:left;
  margin-left:-250px;
  left: 0px;
  top: 150px;
  margin-top: 100px;
  margin-right:10px;
  position:absolute;
  z-index:1;
}
.fixed-page-list .fixed-page-list-content {
  width: 240px;
  height: 290px;
  overflow: auto;
  float: left;
  background: white;
  padding: 5px;
  -moz-box-shadow: 0 0 1em black;
  -webkit-box-shadow: 0 0 1em black;
  box-shadow: 0 0 1em black;
}
.fixed-page-list .fixed-page-list-button {
  background: white;
  font-size: 120%;
```

```
        font-weight: bold;
        text-align: right;
        padding-right: 3px;
        cursor: pointer;
        -moz-box-shadow: 0 0 1em black;
        -webkit-box-shadow: 0 0 1em black;
        box-shadow: 0 0 1em black;
    }
```

4. Finally, we need some JavaScript action to make sure the button stays in the
    viewport of the browser, even when the visitor scrolls down. We also have to add a
    hover effect to display the actual block content. Create a new file called `view.js`
    with the following content:

```
$(document).ready(function($) {
    if (!($.browser.msie && $.browser.version == 6)) {
        $(window).scroll(function () {
            var scrollTop = $(this).scrollTop();
            if (scrollTop > 150) {
                $('.fixed-page-list').css('position','fixed');
                $('.fixed-page-list').css('top','0');
            } else if (scrollTop < 150) {
                $('.fixed-page-list').css(
                    'position','absolute');
                $('.fixed-page-list').css('top','150px');
            }
        });
    }

    $('.fixed-page-list').hover(function() {
        $(this).animate({"margin-left": "0px"})
    }, function() {
        $(this).animate({"margin-left": "-250px"})
    });
});
```

5. Enable the page edit mode and add a new page list block with the settings to display
    the pages you would like to appear in the box.

What just happened?

We created another `view.php` which looks a lot like the previous template we created.
It includes the existing templates and only adds some more HTML tags around it. There's
just one additional PHP element. We check if the page is currently in edit mode, the in-site
editing mode gets confused if we'd wanted to edit the page list in an absolute positioned
location. We simply rename the CSS class to ignore the CSS rules.

`view.css` contains nothing but a few rules to fix the location of our block on the left border of our browser window along with some colors, styles, and borders.

Our JavaScript `view.js` contains two different sections. The first one checks if we're using Internet Explorer 6 in which case, the code won't be executed and the button will disappear if we scroll down the page. For all other browsers we execute a little code when the user scrolls the page. We simply move our element with the CSS class `fixed-page-list` into the visible area using some jQuery commands.

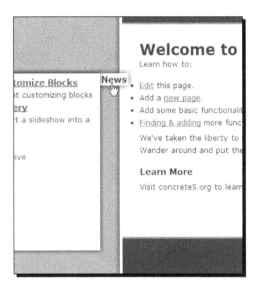

Transforming a slideshow into a gallery

By default, concrete5 comes with a slideshow block you can use to quickly add a few pictures with a smooth fading effect. However, sooner or later you quite likely want to create a more classical picture gallery.

We've already created a template for the content block which you can use to embed a picture gallery within your content. This is a nice feature because it allows you to wrap text around your pictures and therefore provide more information to the visitor.

However, what if you just wanted to show some pictures? Maybe the 500 pictures you took from your last trip to the moon? Adding every picture and link manually would be rather annoying and looking at 500 pictures in a slideshow without seeing a thumbnail is also quite time consuming but adding pictures to the slideshow block is rather easy. Let's turn the slideshow block into a gallery!

Time for action – creating a gallery template for a slideshow

Create a gallery slideshow template by following these steps:

1. We're going to use the same JavaScript as we've used with the picture pop-up template for the content block. Go to jQuery lightbox at `http://leandrovieira.com/projects/jquery/lightbox/` and download the jQuery lightbox ZIP file.

2. Create a new directory named `blocks/slideshow/templates/gallery`.

3. From the downloaded jQuery ZIP file, extract the folders `images`, `css`, and `js` but make sure there's only `jquery.lightbox-0.5.min.js` in it—you have to remove the other JavaScript files.

4. Create a new file called `view.php` in the directory. We're not going to copy the original `view.php` as we have to rewrite most of the code anyway. The following code block shows you the complete content of our `view.php`; it's a lot smaller than the default slideshow template:

```php
<div class="ccm-slideshow-gallery">
<?php
defined('C5_EXECUTE') or die(_("Access Denied."));

foreach($images as $imgInfo) {
  $f = File::getByID($imgInfo['fID']);
  $fp = new Permissions($f);
  if ($fp->canRead()) {

    $fileName = $f->getFileName();
    $picturePath = $f->getRelativePath();
    $thumbnail = $f->getThumbnail(2);

    echo "<a title=\"{$fileName}\"
      href=\"{$picturePath}\">{$thumbnail}</a>";
  }
}
?>
</div>
```

5. Create another file called `view.js` in the same directory. We need it to load the lightbox script:

```
$(document).ready(function() {
  $(".ccm-slideshow-gallery a").lightBox({
    imageBtnPrev: CCM_REL +
      "/blocks/slideshow/templates/gallery/images/
        lightbox-btn-prev.gif",
    imageBtnNext: CCM_REL +
      "/blocks/slideshow/templates/gallery/images/
        lightbox-btn-next.gif",
    imageLoading: CCM_REL +
      "/blocks/slideshow/templates/gallery/images/
        lightbox-ico-loading.gif",
    imageBtnClose: CCM_REL +
      "/blocks/slideshow/templates/gallery/images/
        lightbox-btn-close.gif",
    imageBlank: CCM_REL +
      "/blocks/slideshow/templates/gallery/images/
        lightbox-blank.gif"
  });
});
```

What just happened?

The process we went through is again quite simple and very similar to the picture pop-up template we've created before.

We put all the files related to the jQuery lightbox right into our template directory. This makes it easier to install the template as all the files are located in a single folder. Copy and paste is enough to install this template in a new site.

Next, we created a completely new `view.php` which used a variable called `$image` generated by the controller of the slideshow block. Depending on the settings you make when adding a slideshow block, the controller puts a sequence of pictures in the image variable and forwards it to the template. We simply used this array to print a thumbnail and a link to the picture in the original size of the picture.

Our last file, `view.js` is again similar to the file we've created for the picture pop-up content template. We only changed the jQuery selector to access all links within our `DIV` element and not just link with the `lightbox` attribute.

Time for action – adding a slideshow gallery

To add the slideshow gallery we created follow these steps:

1. In the dashboard, go to the file manager and select all the files you'd like to appear in the gallery by ticking the checkbox next to the picture:

2. As shown, click on **Sets** in the drop-down box above the files. We're going to use a new set of files to access our files from the slideshow block. In the dialog which appears, enter the name of the new set and tick the checkbox next to add. Click on **Update** and all selected files will now belong to the new set:

3. Go to the page where you'd like the gallery to appear.

4. Enable the edit mode and bring up the block list by clicking on **Add To Main**. From the list, select **Slideshow**.

5. In the **Type** box, select **Pictures from File Set**. The interface changes and concrete5 automatically selects the first available set. Since we only have one, you don't have to change it. If you're using the original slideshow template, you can specify the display duration and fade time but since our template is going to turn the slideshow into a gallery, these values won't be used.

6. Click on **Add** to insert the slideshow to our page. Click on the block again and select **Custom Template**, then select our new template called **Gallery** and hit **Update**.

7. Leave the edit mode and publish all changes.

What just happened?

We added a bunch of files to a new set which we then used in our slideshow block. So far we did what we'd have to do when we'd like to add a slideshow. But since we've created a new template for the block, we've changed the template to our new custom template.

After we finished editing the page, you should have been able to use the new lightbox gallery immediately.

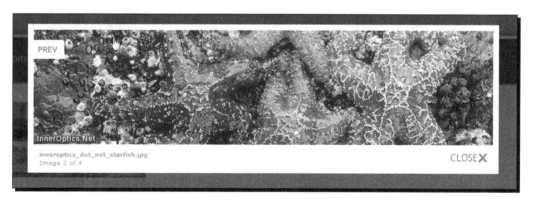

Slideshow using file attributes

In the previous chapter, we worked with attributes assigned to pages. As already mentioned, attributes can also be connected to files. Let's assume you've got a nice collection of photos which are really important to you; you would therefore like to add a note to each picture, telling a little bit about its story. Having this kind of information assigned to files makes it easy for you, to pull them into any part of concrete5 you want.

In this section, we're going to add a new attribute to our files where we can save a little description about the file. We then create another template for the slideshow block which uses this attribute to display the additional information about the picture within in the slideshow.

Time for action – adding file attributes to our slideshow

To add attributes to our slideshow follow these steps:

1. In the dashboard, go to the **File Manager** and select the **Attributes** register on top. You should see the two default attributes, **width** and **height**. We are going to add two more attributes, one for the title and one for a small description.

2. Select **Text** in the drop down at the bottom and hit **Go**. Enter `title` for **Handle** and `Title` for **Name**. Click on **Add Attribute** to add the new attribute.

3. Select **Text Area** in the drop down and click on **Go** again. Enter `description` for **Handle** and `Description` for **Name**. Leave the type as **Plain Text** and add the new attribute.

4. You should now see four attributes. Next, go back to the **File Manager**.

5. Select the first file in your gallery set. Open the **Properties** dialog. Scroll down and look for **Other Properties**. Click on the label **Title** and enter a title for the current picture, click on the little icon with the pen when done. Do the same for **Description** and close the dialog.

What just happened?

The new attributes we created are assigned to every file in the file manager but they don't have a value by default. When filled, we can access them by using a single PHP function, a lot like we did with the pages.

The text you entered is going to be used in the next *Time for action* section. We're going to use it to show some information about the picture in the gallery by using the ad-gallery jQuery plugin from Andy Ekdahl, which can be found at:

```
http://coffeescripter.com/code/ad-gallery/
```

Time for action – using file attributes in the gallery

Include the file attributes in the gallery by following these steps:

1. Create a new directory structure, each directory within each other: `blocks,` `slideshow`, `templates`, and `ad_gallery`.

2. Create a new file called `view.php` which generates the HTML output. It's similar to the one we've created before but the structure is a bit different and we have to access more attributes:

```php
<div class="ad-gallery">
  <div class="ad-image-wrapper">
  </div>
  <div class="ad-controls">
  </div>
  <div class="ad-nav">
    <div class="ad-thumbs">
      <ul class="ad-thumb-list">
      <?php
      defined('C5_EXECUTE') or die(_("Access Denied."));

      foreach($images as $imgInfo) {
        $f = File::getByID($imgInfo['fID']);
        $fp = new Permissions($f);
        if ($fp->canRead()) {

          $fileName = $f->getFileName();
          $picturePath     = $f->getRelativePath();
          $thumbnail = $f->getThumbnail(2, false);
          $fileTitle = $f->getAttribute('title');
          $fileDescription = $f->getAttribute('description');

          echo "<li>";
          echo "<a title=\"{$fileName}\"
            href=\"{$picturePath}\">";
          echo "<img src=\"{$thumbnail}\"
            title=\"{$fileTitle}\" alt=\"{$fileDescription}\"/>";
          echo "</a>";
          echo "</li>";
        }
      }
      ?>
      </ul>
    </div>
  </div>
</div>
```

3. Download the latest plugin from the following address:
`http://coffeescripter.com/code/ad-gallery/`. Download **The whole kit and kaboodle** as there are a few pictures in it we're going to need as well.

4. In our template directory, create another directory called `css` and extract the CSS files along with all pictures from the downloaded file to this directory. The directory should contain the following files afterwards:

- `ad_next.png`
- `ad_prev.png`
- `ad_scroll_back.png`
- `ad_scroll_forward.png`
- `jquery.ad-gallery.css`
- `loader.gif`
- `opa75.png`

5. Create another directory called `js` and extract `jquery.ad-gallery.pack.js` to it.

6. For this template, we're not going to create our own CSS file; we simply reuse the one which comes with AD Gallery. It's not going to look perfect on our site but it works and saves us some time for the moment.

7. The AD Gallery plugin comes with a nicely working jQuery function we have to call to initialize. For this, we create another file called `view.js` in the `ad_gallery` directory with the following content; please note that you have to enter the correct size of your pictures if you're not using the default pictures from concrete5:

```
$(document).ready(function () {
    $('.ad-gallery').adGallery({
        loader_image: CCM_REL +
        "/blocks/slideshow/templates/ad_gallery/css/loader.gif",
        width: 800,
        height: 192,
        animate_first_image: true
    });
});
```

8. Go back to the page where you want to use the new slideshow and add a new slideshow block using our previously created file set. Click on the block and select **Custom Template**, pick **Ad Gallery** from the list and hit **Update**.

What just happened?

By writing only a few lines of code we were able to use an existing jQuery plugin to add a lot more functionality to the default slideshow block included with concrete5.

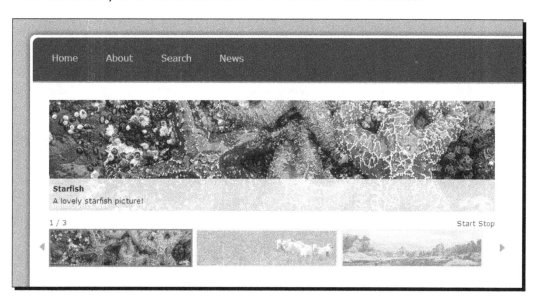

jQuery plugins provide quick, stylish solutions and it's usually quite easy to embed them as most of them extend jQuery with a single function. Some scripts also have lots of options you can use to modify the behavior to suit your needs. **AD Gallery** comes with tons of options to change the animation type, speed, effects, and a lot more.

Right now, with the templates we've created you have to modify `view.js` whenever you want to change something about the gallery. Even if you just want to use the template for pictures with a different dimension.

Advanced tooltip in content block

By default, HTML displays a simple hint on an element where you've set the title attribute. Look at the following code:

```
<a title="CMS concrete5" href="http://concrete5.org/help" target="_
blank">help</a>
```

This will produce the following result, although the exact output might differ depending on your browser and operating system:

Again, jQuery is going to help us to customize this little information box. There's a nice jQuery plugin called **TipTip** from Drew Wilson which you can find here: `http://code.drewwilson.com/entry/tiptip-jquery-plugin`.

Time for action – creating advanced tooltips

Create a **TipTip** tooltip by the following steps:

1. Create a new directory structure for our template: `/blocks/content/templates/tip_tip`.

2. Create a new file called `view.php` in it. We're going to use the previously described technique again which allows us to extend the existing core template:

    ```
    <div class="content-tip-tip">
      <?php
      $bvt = new BlockViewTemplate($b);
      $bvt->setBlockCustomTemplate(false);

      include($bvt->getTemplate());
      ?>
    </div>
    ```

3. Download the **TipTip** source code from the following location: `http://code.drewwilson.com/entry/tiptip-jquery-plugin`.

4. Extract the CSS file into a new folder called `css` within our template folder. Extract `jquery.tipTip.minified.js` into a new directory called `js`.

5. We've added all but one file we need. The last file, called `view.js`, is going to initialize the advanced tooltips:

    ```
    $(function(){
        $(".content-tip-tip [title]").tipTip();
    });
    ```

6. Go to the page where you want the new tooltip to appear. Edit the page and click on a content block of your choice and click on **Custom Template**. Select **Tip Tip** and hit **Update**.

7. Make sure there are links in the content with the `title` attribute set. Click on a link and hit the **Anchor** button in the toolbar; there should be a value next to the label **title**. If not, add one and hit **Update**.

What just happened?

The last template in this chapter works a lot like the ones we've already created. We included the default block template, in this case not by copying the whole file but rather by wrapping the default block template in a new one.

We then added all the files from the jQuery plugin we needed, the CSS and JavaScript files.

Last we had to call the jQuery function `tipTip` for all HTML tags with the attribute `title` within all elements having the CSS class `content-tip-tip`. The class we've added by surrounding the existing block template with an additional `DIV` element.

Now, when you hover the link, you'll see a slightly different tooltip:

Summary

We've created several templates to extend the default concrete5 blocks. While we've only looked at the page list, content, guestbook, and slideshow block, the procedure is the same for every block you can find, also for blocks downloaded from the marketplace.

While templates are very easy to create, they sometimes lack functionality. In the previous examples you might have seen some values we had to add statically to a JavaScript file. This is one problem you might run into with templates, it's just a template, there's no way to change the block edit interface. If you wanted to change values like the dimensions of the pictures in a gallery you'd have to create your own block, exactly what we're going to do in *Chapter 8*.

You can find all the templates from this chapter in the accompanying ZIP file, extract it to `blocks` and all templates will be available.

But luckily, concrete5 is not restricted to custom templates; you can easily build your own block for a more sophisticated user experience. We're going to look at some more templates to improve the **autonav** block, but afterwards, we're going to look at blocks.

Keep in mind that you have to avoid making any kind of modifications to files in the `concrete` directory as it's part of the core and would be overridden if you updated to a newer version of concrete5.

7
Advanced Navigation

In this chapter we'll have a deeper look at the autonav block you use to create dynamic navigation. It basically pulls a selection of pages from the sitemap and prints a hierarchical HTML structure which represents the navigation.

We're going to start with information about the use of the block. Afterwards we're going to create a series of templates for the block in order to change the look and the behavior of the navigation to explain the process of building a custom navigation in concrete5.

Autonav introduction

Before we start customizing the autonav block, we're going to have a quick look at the different options and the output. It's very helpful to be familiar with all the block options as well as knowing the HTML output the block generates before you start extending the block.

Preparation

If you have followed the book chapter-by-chapter, you'll have the `autonav` block included in your theme, more precisely in `header.php` of your theme. Since we're going to play with navigation, we should undo this modification; changing the options in `header.php` would be a bit annoying otherwise. If you're done with this chapter, you might want to put the code back in place; it's mostly to make it easier to work with the custom templates we're going to build.

Time for action – undoing autonav block integration

1. Open `header.php` from your theme; it's located in the `themes/c5book/elements` directory.

2. Since the following code snippet doesn't show the complete file, make sure you replace the correct lines. Everything is underneath the HTML tag with the ID `header`:

```
<div id="wrapper">
<div id="page">
<div id="header_line_top"></div>
<div id="header">
 <?php
    $a = new Area('Header Nav');
    $a->display($c);
    ?>
</div>
<div id="header_line_bottom"></div>
```

3. Save `header.php` and go back to your page. Make sure the navigation is still there, if it isn't go back to edit the page and add a new `autonav` block in `Header Nav`. After you've added it, change the custom template to `Header Menu`.

What just happened?

We had to undo a modification done before this chapter. The code which printed the `autonav` block directly from the template would be fine if your navigation didn't change. However, since we're working on the `autonav` block for a whole chapter, we had to remove this code and replace it with the default code for an editable area.

Autonav options

The `autonav` block comes with a bunch of options you can use to create the correct hierarchical output of pages in your navigation.

While you probably have to play around with it for a bit to get used to all the options, we're still going to look at a few possible configurations which we'll need later in this chapter.

Autonav page structure

The example configurations we're going to look at use the structure shown in the following screenshot. We won't need to tick the checkbox for system pages, which would show the dashboard and some built-in pages. We don't want to include them in our navigation anyway.

It doesn't matter if your structure looks different at this point; the examples are easy to understand even if your result looks a bit different.

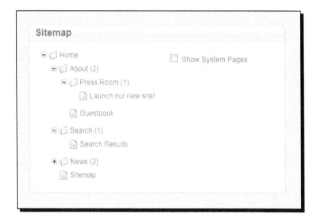

Page order

By default, the `autonav` block uses the sort order which you can see in the sitemap as well. This usually makes sense because it offers the biggest flexibility. Remember, you can arrange pages by dragging their icon to the place where you want the page to be.

In all our examples you can choose whatever order you like; it doesn't have an effect on our templates.

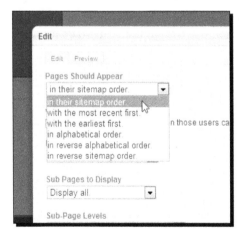

Example 1 – showing all pages

The most basic configuration shows all pages, no matter where we are and no matter how many pages there are. This configuration is useful when you create a JavaScript-based navigation which displays subpages dynamically without reloading the page.

The settings should be obvious and the result as well; it will show all pages shown in the preceding structure.

When you create JavaScript drop-down navigation, you have to generate HTML code for all elements you want to show, but that doesn't necessarily mean that you want to print all elements. Assuming you've got hundreds of pages, would you like to see all of them in the drop-down menu? Probably not, and this is why you can manually specify the number of page levels you'd like to print. Use this for the drop-down navigation we're going to create later in this chapter.

Example 2 – showing relevant subpages

In the structure just shown, assume you're on About, which has two direct child pages. If we wanted to display the two subpages in the left sidebar of our page, we could use the following settings:

Example 3 – showing relevant subpages starting from the top

For a site where you only have a single navigation, probably on the left-hand side, you have to start at the top and include all the relevant subpages. The settings are similar, but this time we start at the top and include the level below the current subpage as well by using these settings:

If you're on the About page again, you'd see all pages on the top, along with the About page and the two subpages of it.

Autonav output

The autonav controller produces an HTML output which is compatible with most jQuery libraries you can find. It uses an UL/LI structure to create a proper hierarchical representation of the pages we show in our navigation.

Before we look at the actual output, here are some words about the process which generates the output. The autonav block controller uses all the settings you make when you add the block. It then creates an array of pages which doesn't have any children—it's a flat array. Unlike what some of you would expect, there's no real recursion in the structure which you have to process in the block template.

How's an `autonav` block template supposed to print a hierarchical structure? That's not too difficult; there's a property called `level` for each element in the array. You simply have to check what happens to that level. Is the level of the current page element bigger than the one from the previous element? If yes, create a new child to the current page. Does it decrease? If yes, close the HTML tags for the child elements you created when the level increased. Does this sound a bit abstract? Let's look at a simplified, not working, but commented `autonav` template:

```php
<?php
defined('C5_EXECUTE') or die(_("Access Denied."));
// get the list of all pages matching the selection
$aBlocks = $controller->generateNav();

$nh = Loader::helper('navigation');
echo("<ul class=\"nav\">");

// loop through all the pages
foreach($aBlocks as $ni) {
  $_c = $ni->getCollectionObject();

  // get the level of the current element.
  // This is necessary to create the proper indentation.
  $thisLevel = $ni->getLevel();

  // the current page has a higher level than the previous
  // page which means that we have to print another UL
  // element to indent the next pages
  if ($thisLevel > $lastLevel) {
    echo("<ul>");
  }

  // the current page has a lower level compared to
  // the previous page. We have to close all the open
  // LI and UL elements we've previously opened
  else if ($thisLevel < $lastLevel) {
    for ($j = $thisLevel; $j < $lastLevel; $j++) {
      if ($lastLevel - $j > 1) {
        echo("</li></ul>");
      } else {
        echo("</li></ul></li>");
      }
    }
  }
}
```

```
    // when adding a page, see "echo('<li>..." below
    // the tag isn't closed as nested UL elements
    // have to be within the LI element. We always close
    // them in an iteration later
    else if ($i > 0) {
      echo("</li>");
    }

    // output the page information, name and link
    echo('<li><a href="' . $ni->getURL() . '">' .
      $ni->getName() . '</a>');

    // We have to compare the current page level
    // to the level of the previous page, safe
    // it in $lastLevel
    $lastLevel = $thisLevel;
    $i++;
  }

  // When the last page has been printed, it
  // can happen that we're not in the top level
  // and therefore have to close all the child
  // level we haven't closed yet
  $thisLevel = 0;
  for ($i = $thisLevel; $i <= $lastLevel; $i++) {
    echo("</li></ul>");
  }
?>
```

The templates we're going to create don't change a lot from the default PHP template. We mostly use the HTML structure the default template generates and only add some CSS and JavaScript. Understanding every detail of the default `autonav` template isn't necessary, but still helps you to get the most out of the `autonav` block.

What we must understand is the HTML structure shown as follows—it's what you'll have to work with when you create a custom navigation or layout:

```
<ul class="nav">
  <li class="nav-path-selected">
    <a class="nav-path-selected" href="/">Home</a>
  </li>
  <li class="nav-selected nav-path-selected">
    <a class="nav-selected nav-path-selected"
      href="/index.php/about/">About</a>
    <ul>
```

```
        <li>
          <a href="/index.php/about/press-room/">Press Room</a>
        </li>
        <li>
          <a href="/index.php/about/guestbook/">Guestbook</a>
        </li>
      </ul>
    </li>
    <li>
      <a href="/index.php/search/">Search</a>
    </li>
    <li>
      <a href="/index.php/news/">News</a>
    </li>
  </ul>
```

Since you're supposed to have some HTML knowledge to read this book, it should be fairly easy to understand the preceding structure. Each new level added a new `ul` element which contains an `li` element for each page along with an `a` element to make it clickable. Child pages within a `ul` element belong to their parent, meaning that the `li` element of the parent is closed when all the children have been printed.

The output uses the default template which adds some classes you can use to style the navigation:

- `nav`: The main `ul` tag contains this class. Use it to access all elements of the navigation.
- `nav-selected`: This class is assigned to the elements if they belong to the current page.
- `nav-path-selected`: This class can be found on pages which are above the current page. They belong to the path of the current page, and are thus called `path-selected`.

Images in the navigation

If you add a new `autonav` block, it will always print text links, no matter which template you use or which option you select.

We're going to assign the navigation pictures as we did with the pictures attribute used in the page list template where we've added a thumbnail. For this we have to create two new attributes, one for the picture in the normal state and one displayed when the page is active.

Time for action – creating page attributes for navigation pictures

1. In the dashboard, go to **Pages and Themes – Attributes**.

2. At the bottom, select **Image/File** and click on **Go**.

3. Enter **navigation_pic_off** for **handle** and **Navigation Picture Off** for **name**.

4. Create another attribute with **navigation_pic_on** for **handle** and **Navigation Picture On** for the **name**.

5. If you intend to use this for all navigation items, you might want to assign the new attributes to the page types by default. Go to **Page Types** and click on **Edit** for each page type. Select the two new attributes and click on **Update Page Type**.

What just happened?

By following the steps in the time for action, you created two attributes which allowed you to assign two pictures to every page. Attributes in concrete5 are very flexible—you can create and connect them to pages, users, and files in case you have to manage object-specific data.

Attributes can be helpful with a variety of different problems; make sure you know how to use them.

Time for action – creating block picture navigation template

1. Copy the default `autonav` template `concrete/blocks/autonav/view.php` to `blocks/autonav/templates/picture_nav.php`.

2. We have to modify a few lines in the new template, and the following snippet shows you the lines you have to modify:

```
if (!$pageLink) {
       $pageLink = $ni->getURL();
}

$navigationLinkOn = $navigationLinkOff = $ni->getName();
$navigationPicOff = $_c->getAttribute('navigation_pic_off');
$navigationPicOn = $_c->getAttribute('navigation_pic_on');
if ($navigationPicOn) {
  $navigationLinkOn = '<img src="' . $navigationPicOn->getURL() .
    '" alt="' . $navigationLinkOn . '"/>';
}
```

```
if ($navigationPicOff) {
  $navigationLinkOff = '<img src="' . $navigationPicOff->getURL() .
    '" alt="' . $navigationLinkOn . '"/>';
}


if ($c->getCollectionID() == $_c->getCollectionID()) {
  echo('<li class="nav-selected nav-path-selected"><a class=
    "nav-selected nav-path-selected" href="' . $pageLink . '">' .
    $navigationLinkOn . '</a>');
      } elseif ( in_array($_c->getCollectionID(),
        $selectedPathCIDs) ) {
  echo('<li class="nav-path-selected"><a class=
    "nav-path-selected" href="' . $pageLink . '">' .
    $navigationLinkOn . '</a>');
      } else {
  echo('<li><a href="' . $pageLink . '">' . $navigationLinkOff .
    '</a>');
}
```

What just happened?

Using the two new attributes, we created another block template. We had to insert a bunch of lines compared to the original template, but the logic behind it is rather simple.

First, we try to get all the information from the page we need—the name and the two pictures. We then build the HTML code to print the clickable part of our link. If there's a picture, we'll use it; if there isn't, we'll print the text as if nothing has changed.

In the preceding code you can see a comparison `$c->getCollectionID() == $_c->getCollectionID()`. This is what checks if we're currently processing the current page. If we are on the current page, we have to print the first navigation picture; otherwise we use the second attribute.

CSS3 hover effect

While CSS3 isn't well supported yet, it allows us to do things for which we previously needed JavaScript. The use of JavaScript would have been possible for most effects as well, but we're going to look at a CSS3-only effect to get a quick impression to see how easy it is to integrate upcoming web technologies. Make sure you're using an up-to-date browser like Chrome 6 to see the effect.

The effect we're going to use is just a bit more than a classic CSS hover effect which you've probably used before. It starts with something like this:

```
a {
  color: silver;
}
a:hover {
  color: black;
}
```

Such a CSS file would display all the links in silver and, when you hover over them, in black. With CSS3, things get a bit fancier, but let's create the new template; we'll see how it looks very quickly.

Time for action – creating a CSS3 transition autonav template

1. Create the directory structure for our new template `autonav/templates/css3_hover`.

2. Our template works a lot like the existing header menu: copy `concrete/blocks/autonav/templates/header_menu.php` to `blocks/autonav/templates/css3_hover/view.php`.

3. Since we don't want to interfere with an existing autonav template, we rename the main `ul` element. In the fifth line, make sure there's a class called `nav-css3-hover`:

```php
<?php
  defined('C5_EXECUTE') or die(_("Access Denied."));
  $aBlocks = $controller->generateNav();
  $c = Page::getCurrentPage();
  echo("<ul class=\"nav-css3-hover\">");

  $nh = Loader::helper('navigation');
```

4. In our template directory, create another file called `view.css`:

```css
.nav-css3-hover li {
  list-style-type: none;
  float: left;
}
.nav-css3-hover a {
  display: inline-block;
  padding: 4px;
  border: 2px solid transparent;
  -moz-transition: 0.25s -moz-transform;
```

```
      transition: 0.25s transform;
      -webkit-transition: 0.25s -webkit-transform;
      -webkit-transform: scale(1) rotate(0);
      -moz-transform: scale(1) rotate(0);
      transform: scale(1) rotate(0);
  }
.nav-css3-hover a:hover {
    background: #e64116;
    text-decoration: none;
    color: #ffffff;
    -webkit-border-radius: 4px;
    -moz-border-radius: 4px;
    border-radius: 4px;
    border: 2px solid white;
    -webkit-transform: scale(1.2) rotate(-3deg);
    -moz-transform: scale(1.2) rotate(-3deg);
    transform: scale(1.2) rotate(-3deg);
  }
.nav-css3-hover li:nth-child(2n) a:hover {
    -webkit-transform: scale(1.2) rotate(3deg);
    -moz-transform: scale(1.2) rotate(3deg);
    transform: scale(1.2) rotate(3deg);
  }
```

5. Save the files and go back to your page, edit it, and click on the navigation block in the previously modified area. Select **Custom Template**, select **Css3 Hover**, and **Update** the block.

What just happened?

Another quite simple template, which looks as follows:

The modification to view.php wouldn't have been necessary if we didn't care about interfering with other navigations on the same page, which would only happen if there were two navigation blocks anyway.

At the end of the day it's only about the CSS file we've created. We will have a quick look at the CSS rules used in the preceding example without going too much into the details of CSS3. We had to use some browser-specific extensions because it's a rather new feature. If you remove those, things are easier to read, for example:

```
.nav-css3-hover a {
    display: inline-block;
    padding: 4px;
    border: 2px solid transparent;
    transition: 0.25s transform;
    transform: scale(1) rotate(0);
}
```

The `transition` property sets the duration for the effect and specifies the element we want to use for the effect. In the case of the `transform` property, the simplified rule relevant when the link is hovered over would look as follows:

```
.nav-css3-hover a:hover {
  transform: scale(1.2) rotate(-3deg);
}
```

Here we can see that the `transform` property has a different value than the one in the first example. It's scaled and rotated a little bit which will cause the effect.

In short, `transition` sets the attribute to use, and will then transform into the value specified in `:hover`. You can also use `transition: 0.25s all`, which would use all properties.

Have a go hero – create more transitions

Instead of the `transform` property, you can access all kinds of CSS properties to create a smooth transition effect.

`transition: 0.25s color` would gradually fade the color of the link to the color you have specified in `:hover`. It works with the location, dimension, color, background, and a lot more; there are lots of possibilities and it takes only a few lines of code.

Drop-down navigation

Drop-down navigations have been around for quite some time. When graphical user interfaces got popular, they were everywhere. With more advanced web technologies available, they also found a way onto the Internet.

We therefore have to create one in concrete5 as well using the jQuery library. There are lots of scripts available and most of them can be used, but we're going to use **SooperFish** by Jurriaan Roelofs from `http://www.sooperthemes.com`. It's a great little plugin—easy to work with and easy to integrate in concrete5.

Time for action – creating SooperFish template

1. Go to `http://www.sooperthemes.com/open-source/jquery/jquery-sooperfish-dropdown-menus` and download the latest version available.

2. Create a new directory structure for our template `blocks/autonav/templates/sooperfish/js`. From the downloaded ZIP file, extract `jquery.sooperfish.min.js` in the `js` directory.

3. In the directory just mentioned, create a new file called `view.php`. We could copy it from the original template and rename the main `ul` element in case there's a second navigation on the page. Feel free to do that, but please take care that you rename all the CSS rules as well. However, in this case we're simply going to include the original template as we already have several CSS rules in the theme which are useful for our drop-down menu:

```php
<?php
$bvt = new BlockViewTemplate($b);
$bvt->setBlockCustomTemplate(false);

include($bvt->getTemplate());
?>
```

4. Create another file called `view.js` where we initialize the SooperFish menu:

```js
$(document).ready(function() {
  $('#header > ul').sooperfish();
});
```

5. If you create a drop-down menu, your HTML code must contain the child pages, even if you only see them when hovering over the parent element. Since JavaScript is responsible for showing and hiding the child elements, we have to make sure the child elements are printed by `autonav`. Edit the page where you want to use the drop-down menu, click on the `autonav` block, and apply these values:

6. Update and publish the page.

What just happened?

A new template based on SooperFish is created. Since most of the CSS rules we created earlier work with SooperFish, we do not even have to make any CSS modifications. The only thing that is needed is the SooperFish JavaScript, another super small JavaScript to load the script and the standard template. Depending on the CSS file from your theme, you might have to include a modified version of some CSS rules you can find in the SooperFish ZIP file. The menu does require a few CSS instructions in order to work properly.

When we created the view.js file, we did not pass any parameters to SooperFish, but there are plenty of things you can configure with this plugin. If we have a look at the example from the author's website, we'll find the following example:

```
$(document).ready(function() {
  $('#header >ul').sooperfish({
    hoverClass:    'over',
    delay:         '400ms',
    dualColumn:    7,
    tripleColumn:  14,
    animationShow: {height:'show',opacity:'show'},
    speedShow:     '800ms',
    easingShow:    'easeOutTurbo2',
```

```
        animationHide: {width:'hide',opacity:'hide'},
        speedHide:     '400ms',
        easingHide:    'easeOutTurbo',
        autoArrows:    false
    });
});
```

An interesting feature other drop-down plugins don't offer can be configured by `dualColumn` and `tripleColumn`. In the example above, any submenu with more than seven elements will be divided into two columns.

All the other properties should be fairly easy to understand—they let you specify a custom animation, duration, and some interface-related features such as arrows to indicate the availability of child pages. There's a nice page where you can play with all these properties at `http://www.sooperthemes.com/sites/default/files/SooperFish/example.html`.

Hierarchical tree navigation

Another variant of drop-down navigation is a tree which works a bit like a file explorer. There are plenty of jQuery plugins for this job around as well, but this time we're going to create everything from scratch. Thanks to jQuery, this is going to take neither a lot of time nor a lot of lines of code.

To keep the example as simple as possible, we're not using any pictures at all. You can surely find a way to improve the layout once you've had a closer look at the jQuery code.

Time for action – building a file explorer-like navigation

1. Create another directory structure for our template `blocks/autonav/templates/tree`.

2. Within that directory create `view.php`, but this time we'll use a different approach. We only want to change the class name to keep the functionality separated from other `autonav` blocks on the same page. We also don't want to copy the default `autonav` block template to avoid redundant code. We're going to replace the `ul` class name on-the-fly:

```php
<?php
$bvt = new BlockViewTemplate($b);
$bvt->setBlockCustomTemplate(false);

function nav_tree_callback($buffer) {
```

```
        return str_replace('<ul class="nav">',
          '<ul class="nav-tree">',$buffer);
    }

    ob_start("nav_tree_callback");
    include($bvt->getTemplate());
    ob_end_flush();
    ?>
```

3. In another file called `view.css`, you have to place some layout instructions for our tree. The script works without this, but the tree would look a bit misaligned:

```
.nav-tree li { list-style-type: none; }
.nav-tree { margin: 0px; padding: 0px; }
.nav-tree ul { margin: 0px; padding: 0px 0px 0px 20px; }
.nav-tree .tree-item-folder { cursor:pointer; }
.nav-tree .tree-item-type {display:inline-block; width: 10px;}
```

4. And finally some jQuery magic in `view.js`:

```
$(document).ready(function() {
  // prepend a span element in front of each link
  $(".nav-tree a").parent().prepend("<span class=
    \"tree-item-type\"></span> ");

  // those span element being part of a parent element get a "+"
  $(".nav-tree ul:has(*)").parent().find("> .tree-item-type")
    .text("+").toggleClass("tree-item-folder");

  // hide all submenus
  $(".nav-tree ul").hide();

  $(".tree-item-folder").click(function() {
    $(this).next().next().slideToggle("fast");
  })
});
```

What just happened?

After you've created the template and assigned it to your `autonav` block you'll have a tree-like navigation which looks as follows:

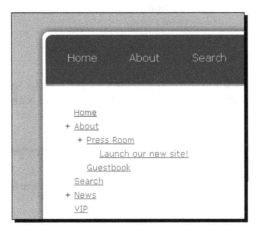

This is another template which doesn't use any external jQuery libraries at all. Thanks to jQuery, we only needed a few magic lines of code to add a small "plus" sign in front of all pages with subpages. It uses three lines of code to hide the subpages when the user clicks on the "plus" sign, and a small PHP template which includes the default template but replaces the ID to avoid any complications with other navigation blocks on the same page.

Dynamically loading content

During the last few years, AJAX has become very popular. It wasn't really new at that time but people started using it more and more and of course, you can use it in concrete5. Sometimes, AJAX is a bit too razzle-dazzle and so is the following `autonav` template we're going to look at.

This demonstration is more about giving you ideas about what you can do rather than a recommendation to use it on your website.

Time for action – dynamically loading concret5 content using jQuery

1. As always, we need a new structure for our template. Make sure all these directories exist within each other: `blocks, autonav, templatesanddynamic_ loadbuilding this path blocks\autonav\templates\dynamic_load`.

2. Create a new file `view.php` with the well-known content:

```php
<?php
$bvt = new BlockViewTemplate($b);
$bvt->setBlockCustomTemplate(false);

include($bvt->getTemplate());
?>
```

3. All the magic happens in our JavaScript file `view.js`:

```javascript
$(document).ready(function() {
  $(".nav a").click(function() {
    var pageUrl = $(this).attr("href") + " #content > *";

    $("#content").slideUp("normal",function() {
      $("#content").load(pageUrl,"", function() {
        $("#content").slideDown("normal");
      });
    });

    return false;
  });
});
```

4. After you've created all the files, go back to your page and change the `Custom Template` of the `autonav` block where you want to try the dynamic page loading.

What just happened?

After you activate the template you can click on a link in the navigation. The browser won't load a new page; instead our little jQuery script slides up the current content, dynamically loads the new page, and slides the new content down.

This works by redirecting all clicks on links within the `nav` element using this selector: `$(".nav a")`. We then build the URL we want to load. Please note that we append `#content > *` at the end of the variable; the jQuery method `load` parses this expression, and only returns the content of the new page which matches the selector. In this case all HTML elements are under `#content`. Before we load the new content, we hide the existing using `slideUp` and once the new content is loaded, we use `slideDown` to show it.

However, as mentioned at the beginning, using this technique has lots of disadvantages:

- We only load the content of the new page and skip the header. If the new pages depend on JavaScript, we don't include the first page as it will fail.

- Depending on the complexity of the content you load, the effect might be a bit bumpy; use it for a personal portfolio page with little content to get a smooth effect, and not your huge company website.

- If you're in the edit mode looking at a dynamically loaded page and start the in-site edit mode, you'll still edit the first page because concrete5 doesn't know anything about that dynamic script which changed the content on-the-fly.

- The preceding script makes it possible to directly link to your pages, but the page address won't change when you load a new page. This however, can be avoided by using a little more advanced script.

Allowing direct links in dynamically loaded pages

In order to make direct links possible, we're using a part of the URL called hash, which we can set using JavaScript. The URL is going to look like this: `http://localhost/#about`. While this still links to the first page, we can use a JavaScript method to check for the existence of the hash and dynamically load the subpage, even if we're on the first page.

Time for action – direct link with dynamic content

1. Open `view.js` from the previous template again.

2. Replace everything with this content:

```
function getLinkHash(linkHref) {
  linkHref = linkHref.replace(CCM_DISPATCHER_FILENAME,"");
  return linkHref.replace(new RegExp("[^a-zA-Z0-9_]","g"), "");
}


$(document).ready(function() {

  // check if there's a hash in the url and
  // dynamically load the page
  if (window.location.hash) {
    $(".nav a").each(function(index, value) {
    if ("#" + getLinkHash($(this).attr("href")) ==
      window.location.hash) {
      $("#content").load($(this).attr("href") + " #content > *");
    }
  })
```

```
    }

    $(".nav a").click(function() {
      var linkHref = $(this).attr("href");
      var pageUrl = linkHref + " #content > *";

      window.location.hash = getLinkHash(linkHref);

      $("#content").slideUp("normal",function() {
        $("#content").load(pageUrl,"", function() {
          $("#content").slideDown("normal");
        });
      });

      return false;
    });
  });
```

What just happened?

The preceding script is an extension to the previously created template. There are two main additions:

- When you click on a link, the name of the page will be sanitized and appended to the URL by using `window.location.hash`.

- When a page is loaded, there's a little code which checks if the current hash at the end of the URL matches a link in the navigation. If it does, that page will be loaded immediately.

When you directly open a page with a hash at the end, you'll still see the first page for a very short time. This is because we have to wait until the first page is loaded before we load the next page. Again, think about it before you really use this; with this addition it works a bit better but still shouldn't be used in pages with a complicated structure and dynamic elements in it.

Summary

We took a closer look at the `autonav` block, an element you'll often need when you work with concrete5. While a lot about the `autonav` block is down to experience, you should already have gotten an impression about some of the possibilities.

The templates we created are fairly easy to modify or extend with some basic knowledge about the used web technologies. The layout is mostly amendable by adding some CSS rules and some templates we've created use JavaScript libraries, where you can modify some parameters such as colors and the number of columns very easily by changing some easy-to-understand variables.

Try to use the template we've created as a base for your own, custom navigation. You've got examples which show you how to include JavaScript, CSS, and PHP to get the most out of the `autonav` block to create almost any kind of navigation you want.

8

Creating Your Own Add-on Block

In this chapter, we will delve a bit deeper into the actual PHP development of concrete5. In the previous chapters, we mostly copied and modified existing functionality. This worked well for basic tasks and even some more advanced features. However, there comes a point when you work with concrete5 when you have to create a completely new block to meet your or your customers' requirements.

Let's get started with a simple block, we'll go through this step by step and add more functionality to it until we get to the end of this chapter.

Product information block

In this chapter, we're going to create a rather simple block, which allows you to enter structured content in order to make sure the output looks identical for all products on your webpage. This block is needed for the second example, which pulls information from every information block to create a list.

While this block is called *Product Information*, it can easily be modified to hold different kinds of information such as: News, real estate, FAQ, team members, and more. The input dialog is going to contain three fields, one for the title, a picture, and a rich text editor for the description. The result is going to look like the following:

Steps to create a block

We already had a first quick look at the files of a basic block in *Chapter 4*, *Add-ons*. Now, we're going to create these files. To do this, we have to create a new directory like we did several times when we created a new template. However, this time we're not going to use the name of an existing block which you can find in the `concrete/blocks` directory; we're creating a new block and therefore have to use a new, unique name. For this, you have to create a folder named `product_information` in your `blocks` directory.

Every block can have a little icon, which you'll see in the list when adding a new block. For this, you can create a PNG picture, 16 x 16 pixels and save it as `icon.png` in the new directory.

Database structure

Most blocks have to process and save some kind of data, which is why we create an XML file to hold our database model. We're not going to use traditional SQL commands to create or alter our database tables. This has the advantage that you can easily describe our model in an XML file which creates a new table or updates them in case there's an older version of it in the database. The file we're going to create uses an ADOdb library, which is described at `http://phplens.com/lens/adodb/docs-datadict.htm`.

 XML is a standardized textual data format to manage any kind of data structure, whether it's a letter, a configuration, or—like in our case, a description of our database structure.

Time for action – creating the database structure

Carry out the following steps:

1. In our block directory, create a new file named `db.xml`; that's everything we'll need.

2. In this file, you have to add a hierarchical structure of tables and columns. The whole content of the file should look like the following:

```xml
<?xml version="1.0"?>
<schema version="0.3">
    <table name="btProductInformation">
        <field name="bID" type="I">
            <key />
            <unsigned />
        </field>
        <field name="title" type="C" size="255"></field>
        <field name="description" type="X2"></field>
        <field name="fIDpicture" type="I"></field>
    </table>
</schema>
```

What just happened?

The file we created is everything we'll need to tell concrete5 what to create in the database for our add-on. Most of it should be pretty intuitive; it starts with the obvious XML file definition, a root element that you have to use in order to tell ADOdb to use the correct version, a table, and a bunch of fields. Not too difficult, but the field types might be a bit difficult to guess, so here's a list of the most common types you'll need:

Field Type	Description
C	Character field, capped to 255 characters. Use this for single line text fields like the title in our example. This field type needs a `size` attribute where you have to specify the length from 1 to 255.
X2	The largest multibyte varchar data type we've got. Use this for rich text field.
T	Creates a timestamp field. There are other types for dates like D but always use T to be consistent with the core add-ons.
I	Short for integer; use this for numbers, foreign key references to files, and pages.

This list is not complete, but should be enough for most add-ons. If you're looking for a complete list, you can go to `http://phplens.com/lens/adodb/docs-datadict.htm`.

 If you want to save a "yes/no" in the database, you might be looking for a Boolean data type. As the SQL 1999 standard does have some inconsistency about that data type, there's no type for this that you can use with all databases.

In concrete5, simply use an integer field and save 0 for false and 1 for true.

There are also a few case-insensitive keywords, which we have to use to create indexes, constraints, and set default values; look at the `bID` field in the preceding example to see how they are implemented. The following options are available:

Keyword	Explanation
AUTO / AUTOINCREMENT	For columns where you need an auto incrementing number, often used for primary keys.
KEY / PRIMARY	Sets the primary key. Compound keys are allowed, simply set this flag for multiple fields.
DEF / DEFAULT	Use this if your column needs a default value. This attribute needs to have a value like this: `<default value="0"/>`.
NOTNULL	Create mandatory fields.
UNSIGNED	Sets a number field to unsigned. Use this for auto incrementing primary keys as there's no need for negative numbers in such a situation.

Keyword	Explanation
DEFTIMESTAMP	Sets a default function to get today's date and time.
NOQUOTE	Disable default string auto quoting.
CONSTRAINTS	Constraints to specify required relations between fields. Can be manually handled in the controller of your add-on.

There's a column called `bID` which you must add in any case. `bID` is short for block ID and is used by concrete5 to connect the proper page version to your block.

There's one behavior which might surprise you: after you've added one block to a page and played it for a while you might end up having several entries in your block table, even if you just added one block. How does this happen? concrete5 allows you to look at or approve an older version of your page. This works by saving the content of every block from that time; concrete5 automatically creates a new `bID` in case the block content has changed in a new page version. It's nothing to be worried about at this point, but we'll have to keep this in mind when creating more complex blocks.

Time for action – creating the block controller

Carry out the following steps:

1. Create another file named `controller.php` in our new add-on directory.

2. Put the following content in it:

```php
<?php
defined('C5_EXECUTE') or die(_("Access Denied."));
class ProductInformationBlockController extends BlockController {

    protected $btTable = 'btProductInformation';
    protected $btInterfaceWidth = "590";
    protected $btInterfaceHeight = "450";

    public function getBlockTypeDescription() {
        return t("Embeds a Product Information in your web page.");
    }

    public function getBlockTypeName() {
        return t("Product Information");
    }

    function view(){
        $this->set('bID', $this->bID);
```

```
    }

    function save($data) {
        parent::save($data);
    }

    function getPicture() {
        if ($this->fIDpicture > 0) {
            return File::getByID($this->fIDpicture);
        }
        return null;
    }

}
?>
```

What just happened?

The file we created is the one which contains all the logic, the data processing. It's still very small, but this is a file which can quickly grow. With this file, we start going into the object-oriented programming. Let's go through the file step by step:

♦   The line with `defined` simply checks if we're running the correct way from `index.php` in order to make sure the security checks have been executed.

♦   The next line is derived from our directory named `product_information`. The result `ProductInformationBlockController` is created by the following rules:

   ❑   Start with a capital letter

   ❑   After every underscore, start with a capital letter again

   ❑   At the end, add `BlockController` to the name and derive the class from it as well

♦   `btTable` sets the main table the block controller has to work with.

♦   `btInterfaceWidth` and `btInterfaceHeight` set the size of our block edit dialog.

♦   The functions `getBlockTypeDescription` and `getBlockTypeName` return a string to describe our block. Please note that the value returned is processed by the function `t` as well. This function is used to translate that value into other languages. In our case, it will return the value we passed to the function, since we don't have any translations yet, but that's okay for now.

♦   The function `view` isn't necessary in our block at the moment. It's only to show you how to pass values to the view, in case you have to process your data before rendering them.

- Save is similar, but not necessary in our case. The block controller saves discrete values automatically by matching the form field names with the field names of the table we specified in btTable. However, if you wanted to save data from a child table or add some checks to this method, this is where you could hook into it.

- The last method getPicture is used because we only save a reference in the form of a number when we work with files from the concrete5 file manager. Since we have to work with this file reference several times, we add a new function which returns the file object and not only the numeric reference to it.

Right now, this is everything we need to get our data in the database and back.

Time for action – creating the editing interface

Carry out the following steps:

1. As adding and editing a block is pretty much the same, we're going to create a file named form_setup_html.php, which is shared by both add.php and edit.php.

2. First, let's create add.php and edit.php; both are rather simple and identical because everything is located in form_setup_html.php:

```php
<?php
defined('C5_EXECUTE') or die(_("Access Denied."));
$this->inc('form_setup_html.php');
?>
```

3. In a new file form_setup_html.php, save the following content:

```php
<?php
defined('C5_EXECUTE') or die(_("Access Denied."));

$al = Loader::helper('concrete/asset_library');

echo '<div class="ccm-block-field-group">';
echo '<h2>' . t('Title') . '</h2>';
echo $form->text('title', $title, array('style' => 'width: 550px'));
echo '</div>';

echo '<div class="ccm-block-field-group">';
echo '<h2>' . t('Picture') . '</h2>';
echo $al->image('ccm-b-image', 'fIDpicture', t('Choose File'),
  $this->controller->getPicture());
echo '</div>';
```

```
echo '<div class="ccm-block-field-group">';
echo '<h2>' . t('Description') . '</h2>';

Loader::element('editor_init');
Loader::element('editor_config');
Loader::element('editor_controls', array('mode' => 'full'));
echo $form->textarea('description', $description, array('class' =>
  'ccm-advanced-editor'));
echo '</div>';
?>
```

What just happened?

Our code is getting bigger but we're also coming closer to finishing the first block. Let's go through all the new steps:

- `Loader::helper` is often used to include functionality from the concrete5 core. In this case, we're loading the `asset_library`, which contains functions to include the file manager.

- Next we use a `DIV` element with a built in class named `ccm-block-field-group`. This class adds a nice little line to make our dialog look a bit nicer.

- The next line uses the function called `t` again, and again, this is just to make the block translatable.

- The `$form` refers to the form helper from which we use several methods. In this case, the `$form->text` method with the following parameters:

    - ID of your input box.

    - Variable to process. Please note, this has been added automatically by the controller because the table specified in `btTable` contains a column with this name.

    - An array where you can pass any HTML attribute to the input element. In this case, a style to specify the width of the control.

- `$al->image` adds a selector, which pops up a dialog to select an image from the file manager. There's another method you can use to select any kind of file, just use `$al->file` instead. In the example, we've used the following few parameters:

    - The ID of your form field.

    - Name of your column. Must match with the blocks table.

    - Text to display when no file has been selected.

    - Reference to currently selected file. Must be a file object and not just the reference in form of a number.

♦ `$form->textarea` prints a plain text, multi-line input field. If you include some HTML elements in front of it and add the proper CSS class, you'll get access to the built-in rich text editor. `Loader::element` pulls files from `concrete/elements` where you can find a bit more about the details of the rich text editor, in case you want to know what's going on under the hood.

Time for action – printing block output

Carry out the following steps:

1. Last but not least, we have to make sure the data we save in the block gets printed on the page. For this, we have to create a file named `view.php`.

2. We've got to access and print the file object along with some basic commands to print the value of our variables. The content of the file has to look like this:

```php
<div class="product-information">
<?php
$html = Loader::helper('html');

$picture = $this->controller->getPicture();

echo "<h2>{$title}</h2>";
if ($picture) {
    echo $html->image($picture->getURL());
}
echo "<p>{$description}</p>";
?>
</div>
```

What just happened?

The last part, the actual rendering of the content, is rather short. We did use another helper, `html`, to print our image element. We could have built this string manually, but which option you choose is up to you. We also used `getPicture` again to get a file object from the controller. Besides these two commands, we only used simple echo statements to output the content of our variables.

Now that we've created all the files, we can install our block. Go to **Add Functionality** in the dashboard of your site and you'll see our new block. Click on **Install** and concrete5 will parse `db.xml` and create the database structure.

Edit a page of your choice and add a new instance of our block, enter the data needed and you'll get a structured output of the three fields.

Checking for mandatory fields

If we wanted to make sure there were no products without pictures, we could add a few more lines of code.

Time for action – adding check for mandatory fields

Carry out the following steps:

1. In `controller.php`, add the following method after `getBlockTypeName`:

    ```
    public function getJavaScriptStrings() {
        return array(
            'image-required' => t('You must select an image.')
        );
    }
    ```

2. Create a new file named `auto.js` that will automatically be included when you add or edit a product information block instance. Put the following content in it:

    ```
    ccmValidateBlockForm = function() {
        if ($("#ccm-b-image-fm-value").val() == '' || $("#ccm-b-image-
    fm-value").val() == 0) {
            ccm_addError(ccm_t('image-required'));
        }
        return false;
    }
    ```

What just happened?

We created a JavaScript, which is automatically included and called before the data is saved. The method `ccmValidateBlockForm` is a built-in method, which you can use to interact in the field checking process. `ccm_addError` adds an error to an internal array based on texts processed by `ccm_t`, which is looking for values generated by the method `getJavaScriptStrings` in the controller. This is necessary because JavaScript strings can't be translated; we have to fetch them from our PHP based block controller.

Adding product categories

We're going to make one more modification to this block before we start with another one. Whether you want to manage products, news or anything else, you might want to split these entries into categories.

For this, we're going to add another table to our block from which we're pulling all the categories to add a drop-down menu to our block.

Time for action – adding product categories

Carry out the following steps:

1. Open `db.xml` for your block; we've got to make a few modifications. The file should look like the following afterwards:

```xml
<?xml version="1.0"?>
<schema version="0.3">
    <table name="btProductInformation">
        <field name="bID" type="I">
            <key />
            <unsigned />
        </field>
        <field name="title" type="C" size="255"></field>
        <field name="description" type="X2"></field>
        <field name="fIDpicture" type="I"></field>
        <field name="categoryID" type="I"></field>
    </table>
    <table name="btProductInformationCategories">
    <field name="categoryID" type="I">
        <autoincrement />
        <key />
        <unsigned />
    </field>
    <field name="category" type="C" size="255"></field>
    <index name="btProductInformationCategories_IX">
        <descr>Makes sure the categories are unique</descr>
        <col>category</col>
        <unique />
    </index>
    </table>
    <sql>
      <query>REPLACE INTO btProductInformationCategories(category)
         VALUES ('Top-Notch')</query>
      <query>REPLACE INTO btProductInformationCategories(category)
         VALUES ('Junk Goods')</query>
    </sql>
</schema>
```

2. Next, open `controller.php` and add a new method which returns a list of categories:

```
function getCategories() {
    $db = Loader::db();
    return $db->GetAssoc('SELECT categoryID,category FROM
btProductInformationCategories ORDER BY category');
}
```

3. Finally, we have to make sure that the form contains a drop-down with our categories, open `form_setup_html.php` and add the following code at the end, but make sure that you remove the closing PHP tag `?>` first:

```
echo '<div class="ccm-block-field-group">';
echo '<h2>' . t('Category') . '</h2>';
echo $form->select('categoryID', $this->controller-
>getCategories(), $categoryID);
echo '</div>';
?>
```

What just happened?

A few modifications to add categories to our product information, starting with the database model:

- A new column to the existing table, which references to the Primary Key of our new table `btProductInformationCategories`.
- The new table with a numeric, incrementing Primary Key.
- A single text field to hold the name of the category.

A small code to get the categories from the database—here we have to make sure the array is returned in the correct way. The PHP array must have the following structure. This is important because the array key (in angle brackets) must match the Primary Key of the categories table:

```
Array
(
    [14] => Junk Goods
    [13] => Top-Notch
)
```

The method `GetAssoc` returns this structure if your query only returns two columns. If you haven't worked with ADOdb before, you might want to look at the documentation first at `http://phplens.com/lens/adodb/docs-adodb.htm`.

Next, we used another method from the form helper to print a drop-down menu using the preceding structure. By modifying the dialog we're already done, have a look at the new dialog and you'll see the new feature in your block.

> If you want to get an overview of the available helper methods you can use to get access to the concrete5 default widgets, you should have a look at the following web pages:
>
> `http://www.concrete5.org/documentation/developers/forms/standard-widgets`
>
> `http://www.concrete5.org/documentation/developers/forms/concrete5-widgets.`

Have a go hero – getting more information about blocks

We've created our first basic block. If you've already got a good feeling about these steps, you might want to dig a bit deeper into the way blocks work. Where can you find more information?

The official developer documentation is always a good start. You can find it at `http://www.concrete5.org/documentation/developers/`. Look at the sections **Blocks** and **Helpers** if you want to get more background information about the topics discussed in this chapter. You'll get more information about helpers during the next few chapters, which you can use for blocks as well as other add-ons like packages or themes.

It's not everyone's favorite, but the actual source code is more up to date than any book or documentation. Try to get a picture of the files found in concrete5. If you remember, we derived all our block controllers from `BlockController`, which you can find in `concrete/libraries/block_controller.php`. This is where you'll find all the methods you override in your block controller. If you're working on `view.php`, you should know that you're working on an object instantiated from `BlockView`, which you can find in the same directory too.

Product list

Wouldn't it be handy if we could create a list of all product information blocks in our website? Creating a list of products or news? Just like we can with the page list block which comes with the core? Sure we can, but we have to create another block.

Handling multiple block versions

However, before we can start building this block, we have to make a few more modifications to our product information block. Remember the explanation about bID at the beginning of this chapter—every time a block content is updated, a new data record is created. This means that after a few updates, we've got more table records than actual blocks we'd like to show in our list.

There are several options to get around this problem:

◆ We could dig into the database model of concrete5 and see where it stores the information about page and block versions. This would certainly work, but as we wouldn't be using an official API, it's possible that our code would be broken in a future version of concrete5. Bad idea, but in case you're still wondering, have a look at the table BlockRelations.

◆ There's an attribute in the block controller that we can set to disable the concrete5 version control. This works by setting btIncludeAll to 1, just like you set the table name by using btTable. This would certainly work as well, but users of concrete5 are quite likely going to expect that you don't break any core functionality like the version control—let's skip this idea and look at a more sophisticated way.

Time for action – handling multiple block versions

We're going to add an attribute to our table to manage the replacement of block versions. In our product list, we can see for this attribute to check if a block has been replaced.

1. Add a new table column by adding the following modification to db.xml; please note, the code only shows a part of the actual file:

```
<table name="btProductInformation">
<field name="bID" type="I">
  <key />
  <unsigned />
</field>
<field name="title" type="C" size="255"></field>
<field name="description" type="X2"></field>
<field name="fIDpicture" type="I"></field>
<field name="categoryID" type="I"></field>
<field name="replacesBlockID" type="I"></field>
<index name="btProductInformation_IX1">
  <descr>Makes sure replacment lookups perform well</descr>
  <col>replacesBlockID</col>
  <unique />
</index>
</table>
```

2. In `controller.php`, add the following duplicate method to the block controller class:

```
function duplicate($newbID) {
    parent::duplicate($newbID);

    $db = Loader::db();
    $db->Execute('UPDATE btProductInformation SET replacesBlockID=?
WHERE bID=?',array($this->bID,$newbID));
}
```

What just happened?

We had to add a column to our block to be able to fetch the correct block version, the one which is currently active on the page. The internal method `duplicate` is called when a block is edited. In order to make sure the old version isn't removed, the block content ID is duplicated before it's presented to the user to make changes.

In your XAMPP Control Panel, there's a button named **Admin** next to **MySql**. When you click on it, you'll directly get to the phpMyAdmin installed with XAMPP. When you click on the table `btProductInformation`, you'll see a screen like the following:

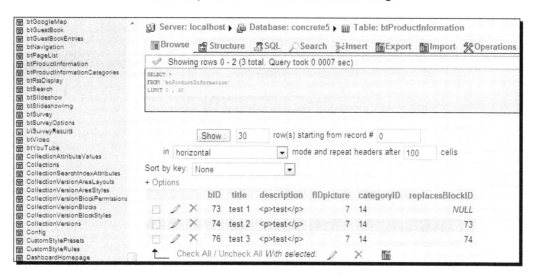

On this screenshot, you can see that the versions 73 and 74 have been replaced. Their IDs have been saved in the column **replacesBlockID** for each corresponding successor. We are going to use this information to present a list of all active block versions, in this case the entry with the **bID 76**.

Creating a product list block

In this part, we're going to create another block from scratch which depends on the first block. It simply pulls information from it and creates a list. At the end, we're going to have a block which creates a simple list along with a link to get to the detail, which looks like the following:

Time for action – creating the product list block

Carry out the following steps:

1. Create a new directory in `blocks` named `product_list`. We start with the database model. Create a new file named `db.xml` in the new directory with the following content:

```xml
<?xml version="1.0"?>
<schema version="0.3">
    <table name="btProductList">
        <field name="bID" type="I">
            <key />
            <unsigned />
        </field>
        <field name="categoryID" type="I"></field>
    </table>
</schema>
```

2. Create another file named `controller.php`:

```php
<?php
defined('C5_EXECUTE') or die(_("Access Denied."));
class ProductListBlockController extends BlockController {

    protected $btTable = 'btProductList';
```

```php
    protected $btInterfaceWidth = "250";
    protected $btInterfaceHeight = "110";

    public function getBlockTypeDescription() {
        return t("Embeds a Product List in your web page.");
    }

    public function getBlockTypeName() {
        return t("Product List");
    }

    function getCategories() {
        $db = Loader::db();
        return $db->GetAssoc('SELECT categoryID,category
            FROM btProductInformationCategories ORDER BY category');
    }

    function getProducts() {
        $db = Loader::db();
        $blocks = array();

        // select all block instances which haven't been replaced
        $rs = $db->Execute('SELECT bID FROM btProductInformation bpi
          WHERE categoryID = ? AND NOT EXISTS (SELECT 1 FROM
          btProductInformation bpi_sub WHERE bpi.bID=bpi_sub.
            replacesBlockID)', array($this->categoryID));

        if ($rs) {
            while ($row = $rs->FetchRow()) {
                $blocks[] = Block::getByID($row['bID']);
            }
        }

        return $blocks;
    }
}
?>
```

3. Create two more files, add.php and edit.php. Both of them have
   identical content:

```php
<?php
defined('C5_EXECUTE') or die(_("Access Denied."));
$this->inc('form_setup_html.php');
?>
```

4. Create another file named `form_setup_html.php` with the following content; it's the actual form which is used by `add.php` and `edit.php`:

```php
<?php
defined('C5_EXECUTE') or die(_("Access Denied."));

$al = Loader::helper('concrete/asset_library');

echo '<div class="ccm-block-field-group">';
echo '<h2>' . t('Category') . '</h2>';
echo $form->select('categoryID', $this->controller->getCategories(),
  $categoryID, array('style' => 'width:235px;'));
echo '</div>';
?>
```

5. The last file, `view.php`, is going to print a list built within the controller:

```php
<hr/>

<?php
defined('C5_EXECUTE') or die(_("Access Denied."));

$nh = Loader::helper('navigation');

$products = $this->controller->getProducts();
foreach ($products as $product) {
    $pageLink = $nh->getLinkToCollection
                ($product->getOriginalCollection());

    echo "<h2>{$product->instance->title}</h2>";
    echo "<a href=\"{$pageLink}\">more...</a>";
    echo "<hr/>";

}
?>
```

What just happened?

Let's go through the last section step by step:

◆ `db.xml`, this file is rather simple. There's the mandatory `bID` because we're linking this table to the block controller. And there's a numeric field to reference the category for which we'd like to show the products.

- `controller.php`, beside the already known methods and properties at the beginning, there are only two methods: `getCategories`, which is redundant to the previous block and `getProducts`, which returns an array of blocks matching our selection. We're not only getting the values from the database, we're using `Block::getByID` to get a PHP object instead because it allows us to call any block method we like.

- `add.php`, `edit.php`, and `form_setup_html.php` are almost identical to the previous block. The form is just simpler since we only have one element in it.

- `view.php`, this file simply loops through the array generated by the controller method `getProducts`. There's another helper, *navigation*, which has been used several times in our autonav templates. We use it to create a link from our page object.

Have a go hero – extend product list

The blocks we've created are working fine, but they aren't really finished. There are lots of features we could add to improve them. It's not part of this book to go into every possible detail; you've just been given an introduction to blocks. Now it's time to be creative and add some more features—a few ideas:

- Create more templates, a product list which prints a thumbnail, and maybe show the first few words from the description

- Add or modify the fields and turn the blocks into a news, calendar, FAQ application, and so on

- Allow the user to change the sort order of the product list

The possibilities are almost infinite; you'll find more ideas in no time.

Picture magnifier

We've looked at several jQuery plugins when we created block templates, let's create an add-on from scratch which bases on a jQuery plugin named jQZoom by Marco Renzi available at `http://www.mind-projects.it/projects/jqzoom/`.

Time for action – creating the picture magnifier block

Carry out the following steps:

1. Create a new folder named `jqzoom` in `blocks` as we did before.

2. Download the plugin from the preceding link and copy the `images` directory to our new folder. Do the same with the `css` directory and `js` but make sure there's just one file in `js` named `jqzoom.pack.1.0.1.js`.

3. Create two files, `add.php` and `edit.php`, with the same content as always:

```php
<?php
defined('C5_EXECUTE') or die(_("Access Denied."));
$this->inc('form_setup_html.php');
?>
```

4. The database structure file `db.xml` is quite simple:

```xml
<?xml version="1.0"?>
<schema version="0.3">
    <table name="btJqzoom">
        <field name="bID" type="I">
            <key />
            <unsigned />
        </field>
        <field name="title" type="C" size="255"></field>
        <field name="fIDpicture" type="I"></field>
    </table>
</schema>
```

5. The block controller also is quite simple:

```php
<?php
defined('C5_EXECUTE') or die(_("Access Denied."));
class JqzoomBlockController extends BlockController {

    protected $btTable = 'btJqzoom';
    protected $btInterfaceWidth = "590";
    protected $btInterfaceHeight = "450";


    public function getBlockTypeDescription() {
        return t("Embeds a picture magnifier in your page.");
    }

    public function getBlockTypeName() {
```

```
            return t("jQZoom Picture");
        }

    public function getJavaScriptStrings() {
        return array(
            'image-required' => t('You must select an image.')
        );
    }

    function getPicture() {
        if ($this->fIDpicture > 0) {
            return File::getByID($this->fIDpicture);
        }
        return null;
    }
}
?>
```

6. Next, we have to create the form used by add.php and edit.php:

```
<?php
defined('C5_EXECUTE') or die(_("Access Denied."));

$al = Loader::helper('concrete/asset_library');

echo '<div class="ccm-block-field-group">';
echo '<h2>' . t('Title') . '</h2>';
echo $form->text('title', $title, array('style' =>
  'width: 550px'));
echo '</div>';

echo '<div class="ccm-block-field-group">';
echo '<h2>' . t('Picture') . '</h2>';
echo $al->image('ccm-b-image', 'fIDpicture', t('Choose File'),
  $this->controller->getPicture());
echo '</div>';

?>
```

7. And of course, view.php, which prints the HTML structure used by jQZoom:

```
<div class="ccm-jqzoom">

<?php
$html = Loader::helper('html');
$image = Loader::helper('image');
```

```
$picture = $this->controller->getPicture();

if ($picture) {
    $bigPicture = $image->getThumbnail($picture,800,800)->src;
    $smallPicture = $image->getThumbnail($picture,200,200)->src;

    echo "<a class=\"jqzoom\" title=\"{$this->controller->title}\"
     href=\"{$bigPicture}\">";
    echo "<img src=\"{$smallPicture}\" alt=\"\" title=\"{$this-
     >controller->title}\"/>";
    echo "</a>";
}
?>

</div>
```

8. Since we've included a jQuery plugin, we have to make sure it's loaded as well; create view.js with the following content:

```
$(document).ready(function(){
    if (!CCM_EDIT_MODE) {
        $('.jqzoom').jqzoom({
            showEffect: 'fadein',
            hideEffect: 'fadeout',
            fadeinSpeed: 'slow',
            fadeoutSpeed: 'normal',
            imageOpacity: 0.25,
            zoomWidth: 200,
            zoomHeight: 200
        });
    }
});
```

9. Save all the files and install the block in **Add Functionality**; place it wherever you want on your site.

What just happened?

If you placed the block on your page, you'll see a small thumbnail and a magnified picture on the right if you move your mouse over it. A simple but nice effect to get a closer look at a picture:

There are two files we want to have a closer look at:

- `view.php`, this time there are two thumbnails in it and not just one. Why? Sometimes people upload huge pictures, especially in times when even a cheap camera can take pictures twice as big as your screen. By restricting the size of both pictures, we can make sure that won't cause any problems on your site.

- `view.js`, first, there's a variable `CCM_EDIT_MODE`, which we haven't used before. By checking this variable, we can make sure that the jQuery plugin effect won't cause any problems with the in-site editing concept. This can happen from time to time. Disabling the effect in the edit mode is usually the easiest thing to do and doesn't cause any problems.

The jQZoom plugin has several options, and in order to keep things simple, we didn't create a user interface for all of them. If you want to change the properties, you currently have to do this by modifying `view.php` and `view.js`. Unless you don't want to create an interface for all the properties.

PDF generation block

HTML and the technologies which you can embed, offer a vast number of possibilities to create almost anything you want. Whether it's a game, an application, or just a website, there's a tool for it. However, even with the growing number of web technologies, printing is still easier and more reliable if you've got a PDF file.

In this part, we're going to create a block which will simply print the word PDF, but in the background, it's going to create a PDF on the fly. Let's take a look—you'll be surprised how few steps we're going to need for this block!

Time for action – creating the PDF generation block

Carry out the following steps:

1. Create a new folder in blocks named pdf. In this folder, create the db.xml file like we did before:

```xml
<?xml version="1.0"?>
<schema version="0.3">
    <table name="btPdf">
        <field name="bID" type="I">
            <key />
            <unsigned />
        </field>
    </table>
</schema>
```

2. Create add.php and edit.php again; the content is again the same:

```php
<?php
defined('C5_EXECUTE') or die(_("Access Denied."));
$this->inc('form_setup_html.php');
?>
```

3. The forth file form_setup_html.php doesn't have any options in this case; it's even simpler than before:

```php
<?php
defined('C5_EXECUTE') or die(_("Access Denied."));
?>
No options here!
```

4. As easy is controller.php, with just the mandatory things in it—no logic or anything else:

```php
<?php
defined('C5_EXECUTE') or die(_("Access Denied."));
class PdfBlockController extends BlockController {

    protected $btTable = 'btPdf';
    protected $btInterfaceWidth = "200";
    protected $btInterfaceHeight = "140";

    public function getBlockTypeDescription() {
        return t("Add a PDF-Generation link in your web page.");
    }
```

```
    public function getBlockTypeName() {
        return t("PDF Generator");
    }
}
?>
```

5. Here's a new element. As generating PDF files isn't that easy, we're going to use a library for this. Go to `http://mpdf.bpm1.com/` and download the latest ZIP version (at the time of writing the latest is Version 5.1). Extract the ZIP file in `libraries` but make sure it's the one in the root, not in the folder `concrete`.

6. Another new element, we're going to create a tool which we're calling from the block; you'll see how it comes together in the next step, but for now, just create a file named `generate_pdf.php` in the tools folder in the root of your site, not in blocks, and put the following lines in it:

```
<?php
defined('C5_EXECUTE') or die(_("Access Denied."));

Loader::library('mpdf50/mpdf');
$fh = Loader::helper('file');

$header = <<<EOT
<style type="text/css">
    body { font-family: Helvetica, Arial; }
    h1 { border-bottom: 1px solid black; }
</style>
EOT;

$url - $_REQUEST['p'];
$content = $fh->getContents($url);
$content = preg_replace("/.*<body>|<\/body>.*/si", "", $content);
$content = preg_replace("/<!--hidden_in_pdf_start-->.*?<!--hidden_in_pdf_end-->/siu", "", $content);

$mpdf=new mPDF('utf-8','A4');
$mpdf->showImageErrors = true;
$mpdf->SetCreator('PDF by concrete5');
$mpdf->useOnlyCoreFonts = true;
$mpdf->setBasePath($url);
$mpdf->WriteHTML($header . $content);
$mpdf->Output();
?>
```

7. Next, we have to create `view.php` to print a link which generates the PDF file. In this case, we're printing a simple text link, but feel free to replace it with an icon:

```
<!--hidden_in_pdf_start-->
<?php
defined('C5_EXECUTE') or die(_('Access Denied.'));

$nh = Loader::helper('navigation');
$url = Loader::helper('concrete/urls');

$toolsUrl = $url->getToolsURL('generate_pdf');
$toolsUrl .= '?p=' . rawurlencode($nh->getLinkToCollection(
  $this->c, true));

echo "<a href=\"{$toolsUrl}\">PDF</a>";


?>
<!--hidden_in_pdf_end-->
```

8. When you print a PDF generated from your webpage, you probably don't want to include all elements from the website. An element like the navigation might be useless on a paper; no one can click on links printed on a paper. If you want to hide the navigation in the PDF, you can edit `header.php` from your theme, which in case you followed every chapter is located in `themes/c5book/elements` and insert the highlighted lines:

```
<div id="wrapper">
  <div id="page">
  <!--hidden_in_pdf_start-->
      <div id="header_line_top"></div>
      <div id="header">
        <?php
        $a = new Area('Header Nav');
        $a->display($c);
        ?>
      </div>
      <div id="header_line_bottom"></div>
  <!--hidden_in_pdf_end-->
```

9. Once you've saved all the files, you can place the block anywhere you want and click on it to generate a PDF.

What just happened?

The block we created has only a few lines of code. Most of the problems have already been solved by using mPDF, which does most of the magic in this little add-on. When you click on the link, you should immediately see a page like the following:

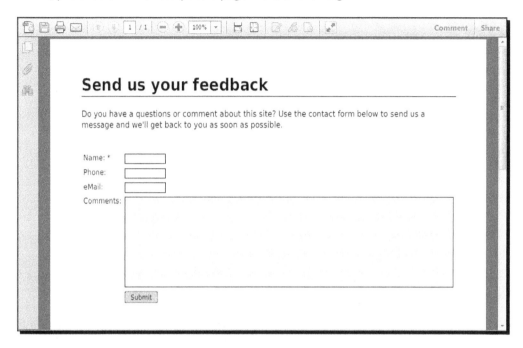

There are a bunch of new files, most of them quite small, but there are a few things we should have a look at:

generate_pdf.php

The file which calls mPDF contains two *regex* patterns to filter the content from the page. The first one `/.*<body>|<\/body>.*/si` makes sure we only get the body and ignore the header, as we don't want to include any of the styles from the website layout. This allows us to style the PDF the way we want.

There's another regex pattern `/<!—hidden_in_pdf_start-->.*?<!-- hidden_in_pdf_end-->/siu` to hide everything between the two HTML comments. It's what gets rid of the navigation header in our step by step example.

At the beginning of the file are a few CSS rules. The mPDF library supports an impressive number of CSS features. In our example, there's a rule to change the font and one to add a line to the main headings, but there's a lot more you can do with CSS.

There are also a few HTML elements which you can put in the file to add page headers or footers, a PDF table of contents, and page breaks. They aren't part of the official HTML standard, and unless you've worked with mPDF before, you won't know about them. If you want to get the most out of your PDF, you should probably have a look at the official documentation available at `http://mpdf1.com/manual/index.php`.

view.php

The block template starts with the comment we already used to hide the navigation. We also use this to hide the link to generate a PDF from the PDF once it has been created.

There's another helper `urls`, which has a function named `getToolsURL` that we use to generate a link to our PDF generating tool. Whenever you want to directly call a PHP file in concrete5, you should consider putting it in the tools directory like we just did. While you can certainly call a PHP file directly from concrete5, you won't get access to the concrete5 framework features, you can't use the models, helpers, or anything else offered by the framework.

FTP gallery

We already created a few galleries on top of the slideshow block available by default. While the file manager offers a bunch of nice features, some of you might still like to work with FTP like we did in the old times without databases.

You can upload files using FTP into the `incoming` folder, which you can find in `/files` and import them right into the file manager by using the little **Upload Multiple** link in the top right corner of the file manager next to the **Upload** button. This certainly works, but what happens if you want to move all the files into a different directory or delete or replace some of the files using your favorite FTP client?

Now we're going to create another picture gallery, which uses the same jQuery lightbox script which we've used before. You can find it at `http://leandrovieira.com/projects/jquery/lightbox/`. You should have a bit more PHP experience in this one as we create a few more lines of code in this example. This time we're going to create everything from scratch and ignore the built-in file manager; we're going to get our pictures straight from file system directories.

The directory shown in the preceding screenshot will generate a gallery like that shown in the following screenshot:

Time for action – creating the FTP based picture gallery

Carry out the following steps:

1. We start with a two new directories—one named `ftp_gallery` in `blocks` and another named `ftp_gallery` but this time in `files`. Putting our pictures in a directory underneath `files` has the advantage that we're less likely to have problems with directory permissions as the `files` directory has to be writable and concrete5 checked that during the installation.

2. The lightbox script files we need can be copied from the previous template, which you can find in `blocks/slideshow/templates/gallery`; only the directories `css`, `js`, and `images` are needed. If you haven't created that template, download the script from `http://leandrovieira.com/projects/jquery/lightbox/` and extract all the three directories from the ZIP file. However, remove all JavaScripts except `jquery.lightbox-0.5.min.js`.

3. Both files, `add.php` and `edit.php`, are identical again:

```php
<?php
defined('C5_EXECUTE') or die(_("Access Denied."));
$this->inc('form_setup_html.php');
?>
```

4. Next, the database table structure, as always, must be placed in a file named `db.xml`:

```xml
<?xml version="1.0"?>
<schema version="0.3">
    <table name="btFtpGallery">
        <field name="bID" type="I">
            <key />
            <unsigned />
        </field>
        <field name="title" type="C" size="255"></field>
        <field name="directory" type="C" size="255"></field>
        <field name="thumbnailWidth" type="I"></field>
        <field name="thumbnailHeight" type="I"></field>
    </table>
</schema>
```

5. Next, we're going to create the `controller.php`; beside the mandatory stuff, there are just two methods in it: `getAlbums`, which is used in the edit form to display all available albums and `getPictures`, which is later used in `view.php` to print the output:

```php
<?php
defined('C5_EXECUTE') or die(_("Access Denied."));
class FtpGalleryBlockController extends BlockController {

    protected $btTable = 'btFtpGallery';
    protected $btInterfaceWidth = "290";
    protected $btInterfaceHeight = "225";

    public function getBlockTypeDescription() {
        return t("Embeds a Gallery in your web page.");
    }

    public function getBlockTypeName() {
        return t("FTP Gallery");
    }

    function view()
```

```
{
    $this->set('pictures', $this->getPictures());
}
/**
* Returns a list of all albums (directories)
* but skips the current and parent folder (. and ..)
*/
function getAlbums()
{
    $directories = scandir(DIR_FILES_UPLOADED . '/ftp_gallery/');
    $ret = array();
    foreach ($directories as $directory) {
        if ($directory == '.' || $directory == '..') continue;
        $ret[$directory] = $directory;
    }
    return $ret;
}


/**
* Returns all pictures in the currently selected album
* The return value is an array of a structure with these
* elements: rel_file, thumbnail_rel_file, file_name
*/
function getPictures()
{
    $ih = Loader::helper('image');

    $galleryRelDirectory = DIR_REL . '/files/ftp_gallcry/';
    $galleryDirectory = DIR_FILES_UPLOADED . '/ftp_gallery/' .
      $this->directory . '/';
    $galleryThumbnailDirectory = DIR_FILES_UPLOADED .
      '/ftp_gallery/' . $this->directory . '/thumbnails/';

    // create thumbnail directory if it doesn't exist
    if (!file_exists($galleryThumbnailDirectory)) {
        mkdir($galleryThumbnailDirectory);
    }

    // get all supported image formats
    $files = glob($galleryDirectory . '*.{jpg,gif,png}',
      GLOB_BRACE);

    // sort files ascending by modification date
    array_multisort(
```

```php
            array_map('filemtime',$files),
            SORT_NUMERIC,
            SORT_ASC,
            $files
        );

        $pictures = array();
        foreach ($files as $file) {
            $pathInfo = pathinfo($file);

            $thumbnailFilename = $pathInfo['filename']   '_' . $this-
                >thumbnailWidth . '_' . $this->thumbnailHeight . '.' .
                $pathInfo['extension'];
            $thumbnailFile = $galleryThumbnailDirectory .
                $thumbnailFilename;

            // create thumbnail if it doesn't exist
            if (!file_exists($thumbnailFile)) {
                $ih->create($file, $thumbnailFile, $this-
                    >thumbnailWidth, $this->thumbnailHeight);
            }

            // build relative paths to files
            $relFile = $galleryRelDirectory . $this->directory . '/'
            . utf8_encode($pathInfo['basename']);
            $thumbnailRelFile = $galleryRelDirectory .
                $this->directory . '/thumbnails/' .
                utf8_encode($thumbnailFilename);
            $fileName = utf8_encode($pathInfo['filename']);

            // create array with all relevant data we have to process
                in view.php
                $pictures[] = array(
                'rel_file' => $relFile,
                'thumbnail_rel_file' => $thumbnailRelFile,
                'file_name' => $fileName
                );
        }
        return $pictures;
    }
}
?>
```

6. The form used to enter the block properties is rather simple if you had a look at the previous examples. There's just one additional part to make sure there's a value when adding a new block, but otherwise it's nothing but standard form widgets:

```php
<?php
defined('C5_EXECUTE') or die(_("Access Denied."));

// set default value when adding a new block instance
if (!$thumbnailWidth || $thumbnailWidth < 1)
    $thumbnailWidth = 180;
if (!$thumbnailHeight || $thumbnailHeight < 1)
    $thumbnailHeight = 120;

echo '<div class="ccm-block-field-group">';
echo '<h2>' . t('Title') . '</h2>';
echo $form->text('title', $title, array('style' =>
  'width: 255px'));
echo '</div>';

echo '<div class="ccm-block-field-group">';
echo '<h2>' . t('Directory') . '</h2>';
echo $form->select('directory', $this->controller->getAlbums(),
  $directory, array('style' => 'width:265px;'));
echo '</div>';

echo '<div class="ccm-block-field-group">';
echo '<h2>' . t('Thumbnail Dimension') . '</h2>';
echo $form->label('labelThumbnailWidth', 'Width (px) ');
echo $form->text('thumbnailWidth', $thumbnailWidth,
  array('style' => 'width: 60px'));
echo $form->label('labelThumbnailHeight', ' Height (px) ');
echo $form->text('thumbnailHeight', $thumbnailHeight,
  array('style' => 'width: 60px'));
echo '</div>';

?>
```

7. In order to get some output from our block, we have to create the standard template `view.php`:

```php
<div class="ftp-gallery">
<?php
defined('C5_EXECUTE') or die(_("Access Denied."));

echo "<h2>{$title}<h2>";
```

```
foreach ($pictures as $picture) {
    echo "<a href=\"{$picture['rel_file']}\"
      title=\"{$picture['file_name']}\"><img
      src=\"{$picture['thumbnail_rel_file']}\" alt=\"\"/></a>";
}

?>
</div>
```

8. In order to initialize the lightbox script, we have to create a JavaScript file which is automatically loaded as soon as the block has been placed on the page, `view.js` like the previous files, directly in the directory of our block:

```
$(document).ready(function() {
    $(".ftp-gallery a").lightBox({
        imageBtnPrev: CCM_REL +
          "/blocks/ftp_gallery/images/lightbox-btn-prev.gif",
        imageBtnNext: CCM_REL +
          "/blocks/ftp_gallery/images/lightbox-btn-next.gif",
        imageLoading: CCM_REL +
          "/blocks/ftp_gallery/images/lightbox-ico-loading.gif",
        imageBtnClose: CCM_REL +
          "/blocks/ftp_gallery/images/lightbox-btn-close.gif",
        imageBlank: CCM_REL + "/blocks/ftp_gallery/images/lightbox-
          blank.gif",
        fixedNavigation: true,
        overlayBgColor: '#000',
        overlayOpacity: 0.8,
    });
});
```

9. It's not really a must but the gallery is going to look better if you create another automatically included file named `view.css` with this content:

```
.ftp-gallery img {
    border: 0px;
    margin: 10px 10px 0px 0px;
}
```

10. Once you've created all the files, go to the dashboard and on the **subpage Add Functionality**, click on **Install** next to our new block.

What just happened?

This time, we needed a bit more time and code, but mostly because of the PHP code to handle the files, the concrete5 related code is still rather small. You can now go to `files/ftp_gallery` and create a new subdirectory. Put all the pictures in this directory and go to the concrete5 page where you'd like to place this gallery.

Select the directory, enter a title of your choice, and specify the maximum thumbnail size in the following dialog:

Once you've clicked on **Update**, it will take a bit of time, since the thumbnails have to be generated. However, do not worry; your visitors won't have to wait that long, as it happens only when you add new pictures.

With the assumption that you have created some PHP websites and applications before, there's really not much in this little add-on that you haven't done before. We just had to make sure our code followed the proper concrete5 structure, which by now should be pretty familiar.

Have a go hero – adding more gallery options

If you look at `view.js` we just created, you can see a few parameters in it, which are static. Using the last three parameters, you could change the overlay color, the opacity, and make sure that the next and previous buttons are always visible in the gallery.

You could also try to use a different gallery script or add a text file to each directory from which you fetch a description. Try to add support for subdirectories in order to allow users to put subalbums in their album to split huge picture collections into several parts.

Summary

We created a few basic blocks; you should have gotten a first impression about the way to build a block. Whether you build simple or more complicated blocks, the process we've looked at stays pretty much the same. Depending on your background, things might be a bit confusing at this point but take some time to go through these examples and you'll realize they all work more or less the same way. You can also go and download some add-ons from the marketplace or anywhere else on the Internet. There are always a few common elements in concrete5 blocks. Once you understand them, it shouldn't be too difficult to use your PHP and jQuery skill to come up with more advanced blocks.

Please note, we haven't looked at every method available, it's not a reference book. This chapter was merely a collection of explanations about building blocks. If you're eager to understand every detail of the concrete5 API, you have to dig a bit deeper. If you don't, just remember the basic elements of a block—`db.xml`, which holds the structure of your tables, `add.php`, and `edit.php` which are used when you're editing the page, `controller.php` for the logic, and `view.php` for the visible things.

For the lazy ones, the complete source code created in this chapter can be found in the `4286_08_blocks.zip` folder on the *Packt* website.

9
Everything in a Package

We created lots of different additions for concrete5 in the previous chapters. The page layout has changed, as well as the block layout, and we even created a completely new functionality from scratch.

While we were able to create and improve a lot of different things in concrete5 without touching the actual core files in the concrete directory, we might have had to manually install several elements to get our functionality into a new site. By using a package, we can wrap all the previously created elements into a single directory, which can be installed by a single click on the dashboard.

What's a package?

Before we start creating our package, here are a few words about the functionality and purpose of packages:

- ◆ They can hold a single or several themes together
- ◆ You can include blocks which your theme needs
- ◆ You can check the requirements during the installation process in case your package depends on other blocks, configurations, and so on
- ◆ A package can be used to hook into events raised by concrete5 to execute custom code during different kind of actions
- ◆ You can create jobs, which run periodically to improve or check things in your website

These are the most important things you can do with a package; some of it doesn't depend on packages, but is easier to handle if you use packages. It's up to you, but putting every extension in a package might even be useful if there's just a single element in it—why?

◆ You never have to worry where to extract the add-on. It always belongs in the `packages` directory

◆ An add-on wrapped in a package can be submitted to the concrete5 marketplace allowing you to earn money or make some people in the community happy by releasing your add-on for free

Package structure

We've already looked at different structures and you are probably already familiar with most of the directories in concrete5. Before we continue, here are a few words about the package structure, as it's essential that you understand its concept before we continue.

A package is basically a complete concrete5 structure within one directory. All the directories are optional though. No need to create all of them, but you can create and use all of them within a single package. The directory `concrete` is a lot like a package as well; it's just located in its own directory and not within packages.

Package controller

Like the blocks we've created, the package has a controller as well. First of all, it is used to handle the installation process, but it's not limited to that. We can handle events and a few more things in the package controller; there's more about that later in this chapter.

For now, we only need the controller to make sure the dashboard knows the package name and description.

Time for action – creating the package controller

Carry out the following steps:

1. First, create a new directory named c5book in `packages`.

2. Within that directory, create a file named `controller.php` and put the following content in it:

```php
<?php
defined('C5_EXECUTE') or die(_("Access Denied."));

class c5bookPackage extends Package {
```

```
        protected $pkgHandle = 'c5book';
        protected $appVersionRequired = '5.4.0';
        protected $pkgVersion = '1.0';

        public function getPackageDescription() {
            return t("Theme, Templates and Blocks from concrete5 for
            Beginner's");
        }

        public function getPackageName() {
            return t("c5book");
        }

        public function install() {
            $pkg = parent::install();
        }
    }
    ?>
```

3. You can create a file named `icon.png` 97 x 97 pixels with 4px rounded transparent corners. This is the official specification that you have to follow if you want to upload your add-on to the concrete5 marketplace.

4. Once you've created the directory and the mandatory controller, you can go to your dashboard and click on **Add Functionality**. It looks a lot like a block but when you click on **Install**, the add-on is going to appear in the packages section.

What just happened?

The controller we created looks and works a lot like a block controller, which you should have seen and created already. However, let's go through all the elements of the package controller anyway, as it's important that you understand them:

- `pkgHandle`: A unique handle for your package. You'll need this when you access your package from code.

- `appVersionRequired`: The minimum version required to install the add-on. concrete5 will check that during the installation process.

- `pkgVersion`: The current version of the package. Make sure that you change the number when you release an update for a package; concrete5 has to know that it is installing an update and not a new version.

- `getPackageDescription`: Returns the description of your package. Use the t-function to keep it translatable.

- `getPackageName`: The same as above, just a bit shorter.

- `install`: You could remove this method in the controller above, since we're only calling its parent method and don't check anything else. It has no influence, but we'll need this method later when we put blocks in our package. It's just a skeleton for the next steps at the moment.

Pop quiz

1. In order to know if you have or want to build a package, you should know what you can do with a package. Try to think of elements which can be part of a package.

   a. A package can contain one or several blocks as well as block templates.

   b. You can include themes and their page types in a package.

   c. A package can contain a maintenance job which is executed regularly for period checks, updates, and so on.

   d. You can include a third-party library in a package.

2. Which of the following things can you do within a package?

   a. You can catch events by concrete5 to hook into core processes like executing custom code up on user addition, page modifications, and so on.

   b. You can create a custom installation method to make sure all dependencies are met before the add-on is installed. You can also use it to add objects needed by your add-on like page types, sample pages, attributes, and a lot more.

   c. You can extend the uninstall method to assure that all traces of your add-on are deleted properly.

Moving templates into package

Remember the templates we've created? We placed them in the top level `blocks` directory. Worked like a charm but imagine what happens when you create a theme which also needs some block templates in order to make sure the blocks look like the theme? You'd have to copy files into the `blocks` directory as well as `themes`. This is exactly what we're trying to avoid with packages.

It's rather easy with templates; they work almost anywhere. You just have to copy the folder `slideshow` from `blocks` to `packages/c5book/blocks`, as shown in the following screenshot:

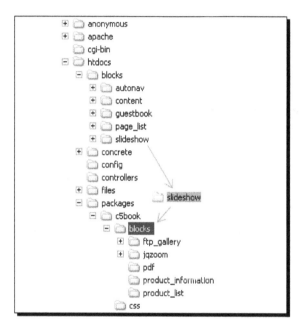

This step was even easier than most things we did before. We simply moved our templates into a different directory—nothing else.

concrete5 looks for custom templates in different places like:

+ concrete/blocks/<block-name>/templates
+ blocks/<block-name>/templates
+ packages/<package-name>/blocks/<block-name>/templates

It doesn't matter where you put your templates, concrete5 will find them.

Moving themes and blocks into the package

Now that we've got our templates in the package, let's move the new blocks we've created into that package as well. The process is similar, but we have to call a method in the installer which installs our block. concrete5 does not automatically install blocks within packages.

This means that we have to extend the empty `install` method shown earlier.

Before we move the blocks into the package you should remove all blocks first. To do this, go to your dashboard, click on **Add Functionality**, click on the **Edit** button next to the block you want to move, and click on the **Remove** button in the next screen. We'll start with the `jqzoom` block.

 Please note; removing a block will of course, remove all the blocks you've added to your pages. Content will be lost if you move a block into a package after you've already used it.

Time for action – moving jQZoom block into the package

Carry out the following steps:

1. As mentioned earlier, remove the `jqzoom` block from you website by using the **Add Functionality** section in your dashboard.

2. Move the directory `blocks/jqzoom` to `packages/c5book/blocks`.

3. Open the package controller we created a few pages earlier; you can find it at `packages/c5book/controller.php`. The following snippet shows only a part of the controller, the `install` method. The only thing you have to do is insert the highlighted line:

```
public function install() {

    $pkg = parent::install();


    // install blocks

    BlockType::installBlockTypeFromPackage('jqzoom', $pkg);
}
```

4. Save the file and go to your dashboard again. Select **Add Functionality** and locate the `c5book` package; click on **Edit** and then **Uninstall Package** and confirm the process on the next screen. Back on the **Add Functionality** screen, reinstall the package again, which will automatically install the block.

What just happened?

Besides moving files, we only had to add a single line of code to our existing package controller. This is necessary, because blocks within packages aren't automatically installed. When installing a package, only the `install` method of the controller is called, exactly the place where we hook into and install our block.

The `installBlockTypeFromPackage` method takes two parameters: The block handle and the package object. However, this doesn't mean that packages behave like namespaces. What does this mean?

- A block is connected to a package. This is necessary in order to be able to uninstall the block when removing the package along with some other reasons.

- Even though there's a connection between the two objects, a block handle must be unique across all packages.

You've seen that we had to remove and reinstall the package several times while we only moved a block. At this point, it probably looks a bit weird to do that, especially as you're going to lose some content on your website.

However, when you're more familiar with the concrete5 framework, you'll usually know if you're going to need a package and make that decision before you start creating new blocks. If you're still in doubt, don't worry about it too much and create a package and not just a block. Using a package is usually the safest choice.

 Don't forget that all instances of a block will be removed from all pages when you uninstall the block from your website. Make sure your package structure doesn't change before you start adding content to your website.

Time for action – moving the PDF block into the package

Some blocks depend on helpers, files and libraries, which aren't in the block directory. The PDF generator block is such an example. It depends on a file found in the `tools` directory in the root of your concrete5 website. How do we include such a file in a package?

1. Move the `pdf` directory from `blocks` to `packages/c5book/blocks` since we also want to include the block in the package.

2. Locate the `c5book` directory within `packages` and create a new subdirectory named `tools`.

3. Move `generate_pdf.php` from `tools` to `packages/c5book/tools`.

4. Create another directory named `libraries` in `packages/c5book`.

5. Move the `mpdf50` from `libraries` to `packages/c5book/libraries`.

As we've moved two objects, we have to make sure our code looks for them in the right place. Open `packages/c5book/tools/generate.php` and look for `Loader::library` at the beginning of the file. We have to add a second parameter to `Loader::library`, as shown here:

```php
<?php
defined('C5_EXECUTE') or die(_("Access Denied."));

 Loader::library('mpdf50/mpdf', 'c5book');
 $fh = Loader::helper('file');

$header = <<<EOT
<style type="text/css">
    body { font-family: Helvetica, Arial; }
    h1 { border-bottom: 1px solid black; }
</style>
EOT;
```

6. Next, open `packages/c5book/blocks/pdf/view.php`. We have to add the package handle as the second parameter to make sure the tool file is loaded from the package.

```php
<!--hidden_in_pdf_start-->
<?php
defined('C5_EXECUTE') or die(_('Access Denied.'));

$nh = Loader::helper('navigation');
$url = Loader::helper('concrete/urls');

$toolsUrl = $url->getToolsURL('generate_pdf', 'c5book');
$toolsUrl .= '?p=' . rawurlencode($nh->getLinkToCollection($this-
    >c, true));

echo "<a href=\"{$toolsUrl}\">PDF</a>";


?>
<!--hidden_in_pdf_end-->
```

What just happened?

In the preceding example, we put got a file in the `tools` directory and a PDF generator in the `libraries` directory, which we had to move as well.

Even at the risk of saying the same thing several times: A package can contain any element of concrete5—libraries, tools, controllers, images, and so on. By putting all files in a single package directory, we can make sure that all files are installed at once, thus making sure all dependencies are met.

Nothing has changed beside the small changes we've made to the commands, which access or load an element. A helper behaves like a helper, no matter where it's located.

Have a go hero – move more add-ons

We've moved two different blocks into our new package, along with the slideshow block templates. These aren't all blocks we've created so far. Try to move all add-ons we've created into our new package. If you need more information about that process, have a look at the following page:

`http://www.concrete5.org/documentation/developers/system/packages/`

Hooking into core events

You've made it through a lot of different concrete5 features if you got to this point. We've changed the layout, added new styles, added new functionality, and even wrapped these things in a package.

However, what if you wanted to react to things happening in the concrete5 core? You want to know when a page has been added, a group deleted, or a new user added. All of that can be achieved by using events and concrete5 will tell you what's going on and let you execute custom code and even interrupt some processes.

Before you can start using events, you have to enable them. By default, they are not enabled, as most websites and website administrators don't need them and would be nothing but overhead.

To do this, you have to set the constant `ENABLE_APPLICATION_EVENTS` to `true`. Open `config/site.php` and insert the highlighted line:

```php
<?php
define('DB_SERVER', 'localhost');
define('DB_USERNAME', 'concrete5');
define('DB_PASSWORD', 'concrete5');
define('DB_DATABASE', 'concrete5');
```

```
define('BASE_URL', 'http://localhost');
define('DIR_REL', '');
define('PASSWORD_SALT', 'DSiBDSPC0wQCa3pAfnhgC8o77rosAFvZAMMG');
define('ENABLE_APPLICATION_EVENTS', true);
?>
```

Event types

There are a lot of different events you can use to extend some core functions. The following table shows all the different events you can catch, along with their parameters described with their number and the data type, and a short description:

Event	Parameters	Description
on_group_delete	1: Group	Fired when a group is deleted. You can add some checks and return false if you don't want the group to be deleted.
on_user_add	1: UserInfo	Fired when a new user is added.
on_user_delete	1: UserInfo	Return false if the passed UserInfo object shouldn't be deleted.
on_user_update	1: UserInfo	Fired when a user is updated, passed UserInfo object contains the updated values.
on_user_change_password	1: UserInfo 2: String	Hook into this event if you want to replicate user accounts including their password (passed as a string in the second parameter) to another system.
on_page_update	1: Page	The passed argument contains the page object of the updated page.
on_page_move	1: Page 2: Page 3: Page	Fired when the page passed in the first argument is moved. Second parameter is the old parent and third parameter is the new parent page object.
on_page_duplicate	1: Page 2: Page	Catch this event if you want to know when a page has been duplicated. First parameter is the new parent, the second one the page to be duplicated.
on_page_delete	1: Page	First argument contains the page to be deleted. Return false to cancel the process.
on_page_add	1: Page	Fired for every new page added.
on_page_view	1: Page 2: User	Fired for each page view. Think twice before hooking into this event as you'll get a lot of calls and probably a lot of overhead.

Event	Parameters	Description
`on_page_version_ approve`	1: CollectionVersion	Fired when a page version is approved.
`on_user_login`	1: LoginController	Fired when a user logs in.
`on_before_render`	1: View	Hook into this event if you want to execute some code before a page is rendered.
`on_render_complete`	1: View	Fired if the page rendering process has been completed.

Page related events are fired for every action on a page. As the concrete5 dashboard has been built using pages too, an event is fired for every action happening on a dashboard page as well. You might want to think if you really want to execute an event for dashboard pages.

Extending an event

The process to extend an event is pretty much the same for all events.

There are different places where you can include the code to hook into an event but as we're dealing with packages we're going to include it in our package controller as well. Open the package controller from `packages/c5book/controller.php` and look for the `on_start` method.

It's going to look like the following code snippet if you've included the event the proper way:

```
function on_start() {
  $html = Loader::helper('html');

  // add advanced tooltips to every page
  $v = View::getInstance();
  $v->addHeaderItem($html->javascript('jquery.tipTip.minified.js',
   $this->pkgHandle));
  $v->addHeaderItem($html->css('tipTip.css', $this->pkgHandle));

  $v->addHeaderItem('<script type="text/javascript">$(function(){
   $("[title]").tipTip(); });</script>');

  // inform about new users
  Events::extend('on_user_add',
    'UserInformation',
    'userAdd',
    'packages/' . $this->pkgHandle . '/models/user_information.php');
}
```

The call to `Events::extend` is rather simple; there are four parameters:

1. The first parameter is obviously the name of the event you want to catch.
2. The class name where to look for the method to be called.
3. The method name which has to be called.
4. Location of the file where the class and method can be found.

Before we create the actual file, we have to create a new user attribute in order to make sure the following example works. Go to your dashboard and click on **Users and Groups** and then **User Attributes**. Add a new text attribute with `ip_address` as the handle and `IP Address` as its name.

Next, we have to create the file which is called when the event is fired. Create a file named `user_information.php` in `packages/c5book/models`, open it, and put the following content in it:

```php
<?php
defined('C5_EXECUTE') or die(_("Access Denied."));

class UserInformation {
    public function userAdd($ui) {
        $ui->setAttribute('ip_address', $_SERVER['REMOTE_ADDR']);
    }
}
?>
```

This little code is called when a new user is added, and once that happens, the call to `$ui->setAttribute` saves the current IP address into the new attribute. This is an easy way to see the IP address for each user who has registered on your website. Nothing fancy, but it shows you how easily you can access objects from the core and add custom functionality to it.

Pop quiz

1. What can you do by hooking into events? What kind of events can you catch?
   a. You can interact on all kinds of actions executed on pages, like creation, deletion, duplication, and so on.
   b. You can add additional checks and disallow certain actions if your additional requirements aren't met.
   c. You can ensure consistency among your website by making sure our depended objects are deleted once the core object like a page has been removed.
   d. It allows you to hack into the core while still keeping the option to upgrade to a newer version of concrete5 without modifying any core files at all.

2. Thinking of real life examples; which of the following tasks can you achieve using events?

    a. Actions executed on user and group modifications, including password changes, can be used to synchronize user accounts between different systems.

    b. Every time a job is executed an event is fired which you can use to write a custom protocol.

    c. You can monitor page changes and generate an e-mail on every page modification to stay up to date with all changes.

    d. You can monitor changes made in the dashboard section Sitewide Settings.

Maintenance tasks and jobs

Some features in concrete5 depend on jobs, which have to be periodically executed if you want to use them. By default there are three jobs installed, which you can find in the dashboard when you navigate to **System & Maintenance**:

◆ **Index Search Engine**: The full text search engine uses the Zend Lucene Search library, which has to be updated by a maintenance job. If you don't execute this job regularly, the website's users will only find old, outdated content.

◆ **Generate Sitemap**: This job writes a file named `sitemap.xml` in the root of your website, which helps search engine crawlers to index your site.

◆ **Process Email Posts**: concrete5 has the ability to handle incoming e-mails. The included community-like messaging system depends on it.

The following screenshot shows you how these jobs look in the dashboard:

Attention: By default, these jobs aren't executed. It's your responsibility as a website administrator to use a scheduler available on your hosting system to make sure the jobs run as planned. As operating systems, web hosting companies, system configurations, and interfaces all differ greatly, no general solutions exist.

For now, you can simply execute the jobs by clicking on the **Run Checked** button. When your website runs on a server accessible from the Internet, you have to set up a scheduled task on that server. If you aren't familiar with that, get in contact with your hosting partner.

Time for action – execute concrete5 jobs periodically

Carry out the following steps to enable the scheduler on a Windows system:

1. Download the binaries of wget from the following URL:

   `http://gnuwin32.sourceforge.net/packages/wget.htm`

2. Extract wget into a directory without blanks.

3. Press the *Windows* Key + *R* to open the run dialog and type cmd and confirm it by clicking on **OK**.

4. In the command window, enter this command but modify the path to wget according to the path where you've installed it as well as the job URL, which you can see in your dashboard. The preceding screenshot shows the URL too.

   ```
   schtasks /create /tn "Concrete5 Jobs" /tr "C:\wget.exe http://
   your-site.com/index.php/tools/required/jobs?auth=9499e773311ba4305
   d5b4b7f35b2c115" /sc daily
   ```

5. Confirm the command with the *Enter* key. You should get a confirmation that the job has been created.

SUCCESS: The scheduled task "concrete5 Jobs" has successfully been created.

What just happened?

The preceding steps installed a task to make sure that all concrete5 jobs run daily. If you want to test the command before you use it, open the console window again and run wget appended by the URL of your concrete5 job, as follows:

```
C:\wget.exe http://your-site.com/index.php/tools/required/jobs?auth=9499e
773311ba4305d5b4b7f35b2c115
```

This command should return without an error and your jobs in concrete5 should all be executed. The date in the column **Last Run** should be updated for every job afterwards.

Please note: The scheduler runs on your local computer, which means that it will only work as long as your computer runs. If you run a website on a server, you shouldn't use your local computer to run jobs periodically, but instead use the solution from your hosting company.

If you want to, you can execute the jobs right now; it shouldn't take long and you should see an updated screen. The number of indexed pages should be higher if you haven't run the job before since we created a few new pages.

 An example based on Linux cron which executes all the jobs 30 minutes past midnight would look like this:

```
30 * * * * /usr/bin/wget -O - -q -t 1 http://your-
site.com/index.php/tools/required/jobs?auth=9499e77331
1ba4305d5b4b7f35b2c115
```

As you probably already expected, you can easily create your own jobs without touching the concrete5 core. You can also put them in a package, which is exactly what we're going to do.

Creating a new job

Jobs are always located in a directory named `jobs` but there are several other places you can find them:

- In the root of your site
- In the concrete directory
- In every package directory

Our job is going to contain a little more PHP code than our usual examples, but since a job doesn't really produce any output, there's not much besides code. What we're going to do has been done before but not nicely integrated into concrete5. We're going to create a job, which checks all your pages for broken links. It doesn't look professional if your visitors click on links and get an ugly 404 error page.

The script is going to go through the following steps:

1. Get a list of all pages and loop through them.
2. Make sure the current page in the loop is accessible by the guest group as we don't want to check hidden pages to keep the output compact.
3. If a page is accessible, we get a list of all blocks on that page.
4. We check the block type for every block we find and skip all but the content blocks.

5. The content block output is processed and every link is extracted using a `regex` pattern.

6. As links can be absolute and relative, we have to prepend the server name in case it isn't there.

7. We then check the HTTP status code for every link and save its result in a table.

There's going to be more than a hundred lines of code; if you don't want to type this, you can find a download link at the end of the chapter.

Time for action – creating a job to check for broken links

Carry out the following steps:

1. A package can depend on database tables just like a block does. The procedure is the same: create a `db.xml` file but this time it's located right in the package directory. Therefore, create a file at `packages/c5book/db.xml` and put the following content in it:

```xml
<?xml version="1.0"?>
<schema version="0.3">
    <table name="btLinkChecker">
        <field name="cID" type="I">
            <key />
            <unsigned />
        </field>
        <field name="link" type="C" size="255">
            <key />
        </field>
        <field name="linkStatusCode" type="I"></field>
        <field name="linkStatusName" type-"C" size="255"></field>
    </table>
</schema>
```

2. Make sure the directory `packages/c5book/jobs` exists. It's where we're going to put our new job file.

3. In that new directory, create a file named `link_checker.php` with the following content:

```php
<?php
defined('C5_EXECUTE') or die(_("Access Denied."));

class LinkChecker extends Job
{
```

```php
public function getJobName()
{
 return t("Link Checker");
}

public function getJobDescription()
{
 return t("Checks your site for broken links.");
}

/**
 * Returns the HTTP status text for the URL
 * passed in the first argument. Uses cURL
 * with a 5 second timeout by default and
 * get_headers as a fallback in case cURL
 * isn't installed
 */
protected function getHttpStatus($url)
{
 if (in_array('curl', get_loaded_extensions()))
 {
  $curl = curl_init();

  curl_setopt($curl, CURLOPT_URL, $url);
  curl_setopt($curl, CURLOPT_HEADER, 1);
  curl_setopt($curl, CURLOPT_RETURNTRANSFER, true);
  curl_setopt($curl, CURLOPT_CONNECTTIMEOUT, 5);

  curl_exec($curl);
  $ret = curl_getinfo($curl);
  curl_close($curl);

  return $ret['http_code'];
 }
 else
 {
  $headers = get_headers($url);
  return $headers[0];
 }
}

public function run()
{
 Loader::model('page_list');
```

```php
$nh = Loader::helper('navigation');
$db = Loader::db();
$g = Group::getByID(GUEST_GROUP_ID);
$linksFound = 0;
$brokenLinksFound = 0;

$pl = new PageList();
$pl->ignoreAliases();

$regexLinkPattern = 'href=\"([^\"]*)\"';
$regexStatusPattern = '(.*) ([0-9]{3}) (.*)';

$pages = $pl->get();

// delete data from previous runs
$db->Execute('DELETE FROM btLinkChecker');

// 1. get all pages
foreach ($pages as $page)
{

 // 2. check permission
 $g->setPermissionsForObject($page);
 if ($g->canRead())
 {
  $collectionPath = $page->getCollectionPath();

  // 3. get all blocks
  $blocks = $page->getBlocks();
  foreach ($blocks as $block)
  {

   // 4. only process the output of content blocks
   if ($block->getBlockTypeHandle() == 'content')
   {
    $bi = $block->getInstance();

    // 5. get all links in the block output
    if(preg_match_all("/{$regexLinkPattern}/siU", $bi->content,
      $matches, PREG_SET_ORDER))
    {
     foreach($matches as $match)
     {
      $link = $match[1];
      // 6. check and fix link to make sure it is absolute
      if (substr($link,0,4) != 'http')
      {
```

```
      if (substr($link,0,1) == '/')
      {
       $link = BASE_URL . $link;
      }
      else
      {
       $link = $nh->getLinkToCollection($page, true) . $link;
      }
     }

     // 7. check link status and save it in btLinkChecker
     $statusHeader = $this->getHttpStatus($link);
     preg_match('/(.*) ([0-9]{3})(.*)/',
       $statusHeader,$statusCodeMatches);

     $statusCode = $statusCodeMatches[2];
     $statusText = $statusCodeMatches[3];

     $linksFound++;

     // we check for 404 and "NULL" which is returned
     // if there's no webserver responding. 404 is
     // only returned by a running webserver
     if ($statusCode == '404' || !$statusCode)
     {
      $brokenLinksFound++;
     }

     $values = array($page->getCollectionID(), $link,
       $statusCode, $statusText);
     $db->Execute('INSERT INTO btLinkChecker (cID, link,
       linkStatusCode, linkStatusName) VALUES (?,?,?,?)',
       $values);
       }
      }
     }
    }
   }
  }

  return t('Found %d links, out of which %d are broken.',
   $linksFound, $brokenLinksFound);
 }
}
?>
```

4. In order to make sure our job is installed during the package installation, open `packages/c5book/controller.php` and modify the install method to match the following code:

```
public function install()
{
 $pkg = parent::install();

 // install blocks
 BlockType::installBlockTypeFromPackage('jqzoom', $pkg);
 BlockType::installBlockTypeFromPackage('product_information',
  $pkg);
 BlockType::installBlockTypeFromPackage('product_list', $pkg);
 BlockType::installBlockTypeFromPackage('ftp_gallery', $pkg);
 BlockType::installBlockTypeFromPackage('pdf', $pkg);

 // install link checker job
 Loader::model("job");
 Job::installByPackage("link_checker", $pkg);
}
```

5. We've added two elements to our package which are processed during the installation. Go to **Add Functionality** and remove and install our package again. This will create the database table and add a new job, which you'll see when you go to **System & Maintenance** again.

What just happened?

After installing the package, you will see a new job named **Link Checker**. If you run the job like shown in the following screenshot, you should get a message telling you how many broken links there are on your site:

However, what if there's a message saying that there are broken links on the website? For now, there's no nice way to get access to that information, but have a look at phpMyAdmin by going to your XAMPP Control Panel and click on **Admin** next to MySQL. Select the **concrete5** database and scroll down till you see **btLinkChecker**. Click on it and make sure you're on the **Browse** tab. You should see something like the following:

We're going to create a nice interface for this table, but before that a few words about the data you can find in the table.

Here you either see an entry with a **404** status code or an empty (**NULL**) value. As 404 is returned by a web server, it means that the domain is available, but the page isn't. In case the domain isn't available at all, you won't get anything back since there's no web server returning your requests, hence the NULL value.

If you found a link which isn't working, you have to know where this link is located in your website. This works by using the cID and appending it to index.php, which would look like this: http://localhost/index.php?cID=64. Using the internal collection ID has one big advantage: Even if you rename the page, you'll still be able to access the page and fix the link.

Anything else in the table output doesn't really hurt and is mostly informational. There's just one thing which you can check: Entries with a **301** status code indicate that the site owner has moved a page and you could check the link to see where you actually end up and replace it. By doing this, your links stay up to date and you save an additional redirection when your visitors click on the links, even if they probably won't notice the difference.

Please note: as we only check the links within content blocks, it might happen that you have broken links in another block which won't appear in the table of this add-on. Due to simplicity and performance reasons, the example doesn't check these blocks. If you wanted to extend it, look for the getBlockTypeHandle check and extend it by the blocks you want to include as well.

Injecting header items

Sometimes you want to make sure an element, such as a JavaScript, is shared in the header of your HTML document. concrete5 allows you to inject any element, such as a JavaScript or a CSS file into the head of your HTML document from your block or package controller.

Adding tooltips for every title tag

Remember the content block template we created in *Chapter 6, Customizing Block Layout* to enhance the custom tooltips with a more stylish version? The template works well, but it only if you change the custom template for every content block where you want this tooltip to appear. Now, let's say you forget to change the template on one page. Nothing would be broken, but the look and feel of your website wouldn't be consistent, which is something we'd like to avoid.

What options are there?

◆ We could create a block for this which would use the content of the whole page. This means that you wouldn't have to modify every content block but you'd still have to place that block on every page.

◆ We could also place it in the theme. This is an easy option which would work just fine but has one little disadvantage. If you want to use this tooltip feature on other sites you have to modify the page theme in order to get the functionality on another page. This is not a big deal but can we avoid this?

We can!

Time for action – creating global tooltips

Carry out the following steps:

1. We're going to use the same script again, so download the TipTip source code from the following URL:

`http://code.drewwilson.com/entry/tiptip-jquery-plugin`.

2. Extract `jquery.tipTip.minified.js` to `packages/c5book/js`. You have to create the `js` folder first.

3. Extract `tipTip.css` to `packages/c5book/css`. You have to have the `css` folder too.

4. Now, we've got to make sure these files are loaded and properly called. To do this, open the package controller `packages/c5book/controller.php` and insert the highlighted lines, as follows:

```php
<?php
defined('C5_EXECUTE') or die(_("Access Denied."));

class c5bookPackage extends Package {

    protected $pkgHandle = 'c5book';
    protected $appVersionRequired = '5.4.0';
    protected $pkgVersion = '1.0';

    public function getPackageDescription() {
      return t("Theme, Templates and Blocks from concrete5 for
        Beginner's");
    }

    public function getPackageName() {
        return t("c5book");
    }

    public function install() {
        $pkg = parent::install();

        // install blocks
        BlockType::installBlockTypeFromPackage('jqzoom', $pkg);
        BlockType::installBlockTypeFromPackage('product_
          information', $pkg);
        BlockType::installBlockTypeFromPackage(
          'product_list', $pkg);
        BlockType::installBlockTypeFromPackage(
          'ftp_gallery', $pkg);
        BlockType::installBlockTypeFromPackage('pdf', $pkg);
    }

function on_start() {
$html = Loader::helper('html');
$v = View::getInstance();
   $v->addHeaderItem(
      $html->javascript('jquery.tipTip.minified.js','c5book'));
$v->addHeaderItem($html->css('tipTip.css','c5book'));
$v->addHeaderItem('<script
type="text/javascript">$(function(){ $("[title]").tipTip();
});</script>');
}
}
?>
```

What just happened?

The preceding code basically replaced the template we created before. However, the new code replaces every tooltip, not only those in the content block. If you don't want that behavior, you might want to keep using the previous template instead of this package controller.

How does the preceding code work? The method `on_start` is automatically called for every installed package during the page rendering process. This allows you to inject code into any page on a website without actually modifying any pages. Do it once, use it everywhere!

> There's a rather simple, but neat, add-on in the concrete5 marketplace, which uses the same technique to include a little JavaScript check to detect old browsers and if found also shows a little toolbar to inform website visitors to update to a newer and more secure browser version. You can find it at the following URL:
>
> `http://www.concrete5.org/marketplace/addons/scala-it-browser-update-notification/`

JavaScript browser fixes

A lot of web designers still make sure their website works for Internet Explorer 6.0 as well, even if version 9.0 is already released. It's painful, but for something like this, a package can make things a bit easier.

There are different projects you can use to help old browsers behave at least partially like they should. One example can be found at `http://www.dustindiaz.com/min-height-fast-hack/` but there are a lot more out there. There's a complete package of fixes available at `http://code.google.com/p/ie7-js/`. What if you wanted to use this for all your websites? You could put this in your theme, but why not create a package for this?

Let's have a look at how easily we could integrate such a browser fix script in our c5book package.

Time for action – integrating CSS fix in the package

Carry out the following step:

1. Open the controller from `packages/c5book/controller.php` and modify the `on_start` method to match the following code:

```
function on_start() {
  $html = Loader::helper('html');

  // add advanced tooltips to every page
```

```
$v = View::getInstance();
$v->addHeaderItem($html->javascript('jquery.tipTip.minified.js',
  $this->pkgHandle));
$v->addHeaderItem($html->css('tipTip.css', $this->pkgHandle));

$v->addHeaderItem('<script type="text/javascript">$(function(){
  $("[title]").tipTip(); });</script>');

// inform about new users
Events::extend('on_user_add',
      'UserInformation',
      'userAdd',
      'packages/' . $this->pkgHandle .
'/models/user_information.php');

// include MSIE fix
$v->addHeaderItem('<!--[if lt IE 8]><script src=
  "http://ie7-js.googlecode.com/svn/version/2.1(beta4)/IE8.js">
  </script><![endif]-->');
}
```

What just happened?

We've included a simple JavaScript file to fix some issues with older browser versions. The same works for different elements, such as a CSS reset script to reduce inconsistency among different browsers. Check the following URLs if you want to start working with HTML5:

http://meyerweb.com/eric/tools/css/reset/

http://www.modernizr.com/

Include one of these scripts using the technique described earlier and parts of HTML5 will work in browsers that aren't really HTML5 ready.

Pop quiz

What are the benefits of using `addHeaderItem` to include CSS and JavaScript files?

a. Using `addHeaderItem` in your package or block controller makes sure the elements are included in the head of your HTML document.

b. Putting CSS files in the header allows the page to render progressively, which can improve the user experience.

c. CSS and JavaScript files are easier to cache if they are saved in an external file which is included by `addHeaderItem`.

d. All of the above.

Have a go hero – create a new package

We've included a lot of functionality in a single package. This simplifies a few things because we don't have to create new packages all the time, but it comes at a price—unnecessary overhead.

Try to move some of the created functionality into new packages. Having a package for a single JavaScript fix seems a bit extreme as it contains some overhead, but is easier to work with, as installing an additional package is only a matter of seconds.

Summary

In this chapter, you should have learned about the things we can do with a package. We started by moving some of our previous add-ons into a package, making it easier to handle and install. Creating a package is often about the installation process, which is one reason why you have to wrap add-ons in a package if you want to publish them on the concrete5 marketplace.

We also had a quick look at events, a nice but advanced feature that you can use to execute custom code upon certain events happening in the concrete5 core. An example: Being able to hook into actions happening on your user database allows you to synchronize accounts with another system. Think about third-party forum software you want to use—if you already have a concrete5 website, you could create an interface to keep both user databases up to date without needing your website's users to register twice.

Next, we created a maintenance job, which checks for broken links on your website. This was just one example. Maintenance jobs or tasks can be used to optimize databases, index pages, start an interface, and a lot more.

At the end of the chapter, we looked at a way to include JavaScripts in the header of every page—a simple but effective way to include JavaScripts to improve the look and usability as well as compatibility with older browsers.

10
Dashboard Extensions

In this chapter, we're going to look at extensions which add more reports, and functions to the dashboard. As concrete5 uses the MVC pattern to do this, we're also going to have a quick look at the theory behind this pattern. However, due to the targeted audience, we're only going to scratch the surface of the topic, in order to assure that a PHP programmer who hasn't worked with MVC before gets enough information to understand the pattern and use it in concrete5.

MVC—model view controller

You might not have noticed, but we did use parts of the MVC pattern before when we built our first block. A block consists of a controller located in a file named `controller.php` and a view, by default named `view.php`. There can also be more views in the `templates` directory, which are called custom block templates in concrete5.

In concrete5, most pages are created from a page type. It's what you mostly do when you add a new page in the sitemap, but there are single pages like `/login` and `/dashboard` as well. Their functionality is usually unique, thus they are called single pages. A single page is what we're going to create when we output from an application in concrete5, which follows the MVC pattern.

Why MVC? What are the problems MVC tries to solve?

- ◆ Different elements of the application have been included in a single file, the application logic, as well as the layout. There's no obvious structure in the application, making it hard to get a clear understanding of it.

- ◆ MVC allows different outputs for different devices, such as mobile phones.

- It's hard to assign tasks to different people if there's no common structure in the application. Without following a pattern, it's not clear which files have to be modified when changing the database access, layout, or logic of the application.

- Modularizing the application was tricky. Modifying a single part (logic, output, and model) has been more time consuming than necessary.

There are different approaches to achieve these things, but MVC has proven to be a solid and popular choice for lots of web, as well as desktop-applications.

How does the MVC pattern do this? It does this mostly by splitting the view (output), the model (database access), and controller (logic, parsing, and so on) into different files. This helps to keep a clean structure in your application. This makes it easier for a new developer to understand your application, even if he hasn't worked with it before. The following graphic illustrates how these units work together. There are some additional elements to explain the use of these MVC elements:

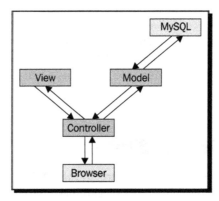

Don't expect that an application will follow this MVC pattern in every case. There's sometimes a situation where you'll have to break the pattern, but there has to be a good reason for that. Don't give up the pattern too quickly; it's worth the effort.

Let's look at some situations which might happen during the lifecycle of a web application and their solutions when working with MVC. If you ever created PHP applications where you had the logic, database access, and output in one file, think how you'd have done that.

- **Database tuning**: Let's assume your application doesn't perform anymore. You get a database expert who knows everything about the database you're using, but there are some queries he cannot tune without rewriting the query. By using a model, he'll quickly get access to the query without having to read through lots of code related to the business logic or output of your application, there's no HTML, AJAX, or CSS interfering with the database access. He can use his full skills without wasting any time on things he's not familiar with.

- ◆ **Mobile phone layout**: On a lovely Monday morning, two days before the project deadline, your boss tells you that the customer realized that the stunning web application you created doesn't work on his kid's Smartphone. Thankfully, you're using MVC and don't have to recreate the whole application; you just have to add another view to your application, add a check to detect mobile devices, and switch to that layout (or theme in the case of concrete5).

- ◆ **New layout**: Your new co-worker has to redesign the application. The super-fast, flexible, and smart application you created 10 years ago doesn't look good enough for the marketing department anymore. As you're too busy with the new configuration management, you don't have enough time to teach your co-worker about the inner-workings of your application. You also want to make sure that he doesn't screw up the core of your application. Thankfully, you're using MVC and only have to give him access to the views and not the models or controllers.

Can you see how MVC can make your life a lot easier? Splitting an application into different files and objects allows you to use the skills of people the right way and keeps your application more solid, extendable, easier to test, read, and maintain.

Broken link interface

In order to easily understand how this interface works, the first example has been over simplified. The maintenance job we created in previous chapter searches for links in our website and checks if they are still working. However, there's no interface in the dashboard yet. We're going to use the data from the link checker job as a basis for our first dashboard extension. We are starting with a controller and a single page (view), but no model for now. We're going to add that later in this chapter.

At the end we're going to have an additional child page underneath **Reports** where the broken links are listed, as shown in the following screenshot:

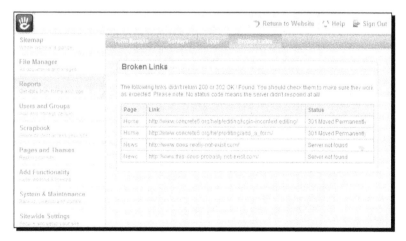

Time for action – creating the broken links dashboard extension

Carry out the following steps:

1. In our package c5book, create a new directory structure controllers/
dashboard/reports.

2. Within the new directory, create a file named broken_links.php and put the
following content in it to fetch the data, and pass it on to the single page by using
$this->set:

```php
<?php
defined('C5_EXECUTE') or die(_("Access Denied."));

class DashboardReportsBrokenLinksController extends Controller {

    public $helpers = array('form', 'html');

    public function view() {
        $db = Loader::db();

        $brokenLinks = array();
        $result = $db->Execute('SELECT * FROM btLinkChecker WHERE
        linkStatusCode NOT IN (200,302) OR linkStatusCode IS NULL');
        while ($row = $result->FetchRow()) {
            $row['page'] = Page::getByID($row['cID']);
            $row['status'] = $row['linkStatusCode'] . ' ' .
            $row['linkStatusName'];
            if (trim($row['status']) == '')
            $row['status'] = 'Server not found';
            $brokenLinks[] = $row;
        }
        $this->set('links', $brokenLinks);
    }

}
?>
```

3. In our package c5book, create a new directory structure single_pages/
dashboard/reports.

4. Create a new file using the same name you've used for the controller and add the following lines to it:

```php
<?php
defined('C5_EXECUTE') or die(_("Access Denied."));
?>
<h1><span><?php echo t('Broken Links')?></span></h1>
<div class="ccm-dashboard-inner">

  <p><?php echo t('The following links didn\'t return 200 or 302
  OK / Found. You should check them to make sure they work as
  expected. Please note: No status code means the server didn\'t
  respond at all!')?></p>

  <table class="entry-form" >
   <tr>
    <td class="header">Page</td>
    <td class="header">Link</td>
    <td class="header">Status</td>
   </tr>
   <?php foreach ($links as $link): ?>
    <tr>
     <td>
      <a target="_blank" href="<?php echo $link['page']->
       getCollectionPath()?>/">
      <?php echo $link['page']->getCollectionName()?>
      </a>
     </td>
     <td>
      <a target="_blank" href="<?php echo $link['link']?>">
      <?php echo $link['link']?>
      </a>
     </td>
     <td>
      <?php echo $link['status']?>
     </td>
    </tr>
    <?php endforeach; ?>
   </table>

</div>
```

5. Single pages aren't automatically installed with the package, we have to modify our package controller to achieve this. Open `packages/c5book/controller.php` and look for the method `install` and insert the highlighted lines:

```
public function install() {
    $pkg = parent::install();

    // install blocks
    BlockType::installBlockTypeFromPackage('jqzoom', $pkg);
    BlockType::installBlockTypeFromPackage('product_information',
     $pkg);
    BlockType::installBlockTypeFromPackage('product_list', $pkg);
    BlockType::installBlockTypeFromPackage('ftp_gallery', $pkg);
    BlockType::installBlockTypeFromPackage('pdf', $pkg);

    // install link checker job
    Loader::model("job");
    Job::installByPackage("link_checker", $pkg);

    // install single pages
    Loader::model('single_page');
    SinglePage::add('/dashboard/reports/broken_links', $pkg);
}
```

6. Go to your dashboard and click on **Add Functionality** and select your package, then uninstall and reinstall it.

What just happened?

After you reinstall our package, you should be able to see the new page when you click on **Reports** in your dashboard, as shown in the preceding screenshot. If you look at the installer, you can see that we've added our own page at `/dashboard/reports/broken_links`. How do you know that path? A dashboard extension is basically a single page located in the right structure. We could have placed our page in the top level and it would appear within our own website using our own theme, but since we placed it underneath dashboard, it automatically looks and behaves like a dashboard page. You can easily get the details about the dashboard structure by navigating to the sitemap and tick the checkbox `Show System Pages`.

Whenever you run the maintenance job Link Checker, you should see an updated list of broken links in this additional report. Please don't forget, that the job won't run automatically unless you use a scheduler like cron.

The example we created has been simplified to show you a first partial MVC example. The controller we created, which of course can be found in the `controllers` directory, is responsible for fetching the data from our database, something which should actually happen in the model. We're going to split this part into a model to comply with all the MVC parts right after this block.

In our controller, we've got only one method named `view`. This is a method which is automatically called by the controller upon a page view if there's no other method specified. We then use `$this->set` to pass a value to our single page. If you call `$this->set('weather', 'Lovely & Sunny')`, you can access the content of weather in the single page, as if it was a local variable with a command like `echo $weather`. This works with discrete values, but also with objects or an array like we did in our example.

The output, our single page is rather simple; it basically creates a loop over the array generated in the controller and prints a table. Nothing fancy, just a loop with a few concrete5 methods to get the values of the object the right way.

Moving database access into model

As mentioned before, the database access should be encapsulated in a model in order to make sure all database access can be found in the same place. While you'll probably find a lot of examples in the wild where all database access is in the controller, we have to create a model if we want to follow every part of MVC properly.

You'll see that the extra effort is rather small; it's no big deal to create a model, even if there's just a single method in it.

Time for action – creating package model

Carry out the following steps:

1. In our package c5book, create a new folder named `models` if it doesn't already exist. Within that folder, create a new file named `broken_links.php`.

```php
<?php
defined('C5_EXECUTE') or die(_("Access Denied."));

class BrokenLinks {
  public static function add($cID, $link, $statusCode,
  $statusName) {
      $db = Loader::db();

      $values = array($cID, $link, $statusCode, $statusName);
      $db->Execute('INSERT INTO btLinkChecker (cID, link,
      linkStatusCode, linkStatusName) VALUES (?,?,?,?)', $values);
```

```
    }

    public static function deleteAll() {
        $db = Loader::db();

        $db->Execute('DELETE FROM btLinkChecker');
    }

    public static function getBrokenLinks($includeDetails=true) {
        $query = 'SELECT * FROM btLinkChecker WHERE linkStatusCode
        NOT IN (200,302) OR linkStatusCode IS NULL';
        return BrokenLinks::getLinksInternal(
        $query, $includeDetails);
    }

    public static function getAllLinks($includeDetails=true) {
        $query = 'SELECT * FROM btLinkChecker';
        return BrokenLinks::getLinksInternal(
        $query, $includeDetails);
    }


    private static function getLinksInternal($query,
    $includeDetails=true) {

        $db = Loader::db();

        $brokenLinks = array();
        $result = $db->Execute($query);
        while ($row = $result->FetchRow()) {
            if ($includeDetails) {
                $row['page'] = Page::getByID($row['cID']);
                $row['status'] = $row['linkStatusCode'] . ' ' .
                $row['linkStatusName'];
                if (trim($row['status']) == '')
                $row['status'] = 'Server not found';
            }

            $brokenLinks[] = $row;
        }

        return $brokenLinks;
    }
}
?>
```

2. Next, we have to make sure our controller uses the model and doesn't contain any SQL queries, open `packages/c5book/controllers/dashboard/reports/broken_links.php` again and make sure it looks like the following:

```php
<?php
defined('C5_EXECUTE') or die(_("Access Denied."));

class DashboardReportsBrokenLinksController extends Controller {

    public $helpers = array('form', 'html');

    public function view() {

        Loader::model('broken_links', 'c5book');
        $this->set('links', BrokenLinks::getBrokenLinks());

    }

}
?>
```

3. The maintenance job we've already created contains some SQL statements as well; open `packages/c5book/jobs/link_checker.php` and modify the run method to match the following code (the changed lines are highlighted):

```php
public function run()
{
 Loader::model('page_list');
 Loader::model('broken_links', 'c5book');

 $nh = Loader::helper('navigation');
 $db = Loader::db();
 $g = Group::getByID(GUEST_GROUP_ID);
 $linksFound = 0;
 $brokenLinksFound = 0;

 $pl = new PageList();
 $pl->ignoreAliases();

 $regexLinkPattern = 'href=\"([^\"]*)\"';
 $regexStatusPattern = '(.*) ([0-9]{3}) (.*)';

 $pages = $pl->get();
```

```
// delete data from previous runs
BrokenLinks::deleteAll();


// 1. get all pages
foreach ($pages as $page)
{

 // 2. check permission
 $g->setPermissionsForObject($page);
 if ($g->canRead())
 {
  $collectionPath = $page->getCollectionPath();

  // 3. get all blocks
  $blocks = $page->getBlocks();
  foreach ($blocks as $block)
  {

   // 4. only process the output of content blocks
   if ($block->getBlockTypeHandle() == 'content')
   {
    $bi = $block->getInstance();

    // 5. get all links in the block output
    if(preg_match_all("/{$regexLinkPattern}/siU", $bi->content,
      $matches, PREG_SET_ORDER))
    {
     foreach($matches as $match)
     {
      $link = $match[1];

      // 6. check and fix link to make sure they are absolute
      if (substr($link,0,4) != 'http')
      {
       if (substr($link,0,1) == '/')
       {
        $link = BASE_URL . $link;
       }
       else
       {
        $link = $nh->getLinkToCollection($page, true) . $link;
       }
      }
```

```
// 7. check link status and save it in btLinkChecker
statusHeader = $this->getHttpStatus($link);
preg_match('/(.*) ([0-9]{3})(.*)/',
  $statusHeader,$statusCodeMatches);

$statusCode = $statusCodeMatches[2];
$statusText = $statusCodeMatches[3];

$linksFound++;

// we check for 404 and "NULL" which is returned
// if there's no webserver responding. 404 is
// only returned by a running webserver
if ($statusCode == '404' || !$statusCode)
{
 $brokenLinksFound++;
}

BrokenLinks::add($page->getCollectionID(), $link,
 $statusCode, $statusText);

        }
       }
      }
     }
    }
   }

 return t('Found %d links, out of which %d are broken.',
  $linksFound, $brokenLinksFound);
}
```

4. Save all the files and run the job again. It works as if nothing has changed.

What just happened?

The changes we made won't be noticed by a person using the website, the output is still the same. All changes are in the background and only improve the readability of the code by following the MVC pattern.

Remember the example at the beginning of this chapter about database tuning? If you happen to run into a database performance issue, you can quickly send someone your model and it's quite clear what kind of requests you run on the database.

A few words about the number of executions per method and your database expert can tune your application on the database side without knowing a lot of concrete5 or PHP.

The first MVC example is done. There are no interactions and no advanced features, but it already contains every element of MVC. At this point, we're just going to add more features to our files, but we're not going to add new parts such as models, controllers, or views.

Multiple controller methods

In the previous example, we used the `view` method to access our data and pass it on to the single page. This method is the default method which is called when you open your page like `http://localhost/index.php/dashboard/reports/broken_links/`.

If we want to add a second method to display all links, not only the broken ones, we can easily add a new method to our controller. The previously created model contains two methods, `getBrokenLinks` which we already use and `getAllLinks` which simply returns all links found in the content blocks not only the broken ones.

All we have to do is to add a second controller method to switch between the two methods and add some basic code to the single page.

The following illustration shows the way the URL is mapped to a controller method. By default, concrete5 is going to call the `view` method if the URL is ended with a controller. However, if you append a method name, concrete5 will look for a method with that name in the controller.

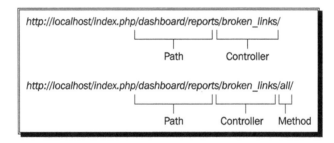

The preceding illustration maps the following controller code:

```php
<?php
defined('C5_EXECUTE') or die(_("Access Denied."));

class DashboardReportsBrokenLinksController extends Controller {

    public $helpers = array('form', 'html');

    public function view() {
        Loader::model('broken_links', 'c5book');
```

```
        $this->set('mode', 'brokenLinks');
        $this->set('links', BrokenLinks::getBrokenLinks());
    }

    public function all() {
        Loader::model('broken_links', 'c5book');

        $this->set('mode', 'allLinks');
        $this->set('links', BrokenLinks::getAllLinks());
    }
}
?>
```

Time for action – adding a second controller method

Carry out the following steps:

1. Open the controller again `packages/c5book/controllers/dashboard/reports/broken_links.php` and put the preceding code in it. It's pretty much the same, except there's a second method in it to display all links.

2. The output, our single page, needs to handle these two modes as well. We're going to display a different text and a different link to switch between the two modes. We're using the variable `mode`, which is set to a different value by the two controller methods. Open `packages/c5book/single_pages/dashboard/reports/broken_links.php` and alter the content to match the following:

```
<?php
defined('C5_EXECUTE') or die(_("Access Denied."));
?>
<h1><span><?php echo t('Broken Links')?></span></h1>
<div class="ccm-dashboard-inner">

  <?php if ($mode == 'brokenLinks'): ?>
  <p><?php echo t('The following links didn\'t return 200 or 302 OK
    / Found. You should check them to make sure they work as
      expected. Please note: No status code means the server
      didn\'t respond at all!')?>
  </p>

  <p>
   <a href="<?php echo $this->url
     ('/dashboard/reports/broken_links', 'all')?>">Show All Links
   </a>
  </p>
```

```php
<?php else: ?>
<p><?php echo t('These are all the links found in the content
    blocks of your site. Click on the link below to display broken
    links only.')?>
</p>

<p>
 <a href="<?php echo $this->url
    ('/dashboard/reports/broken_links')?>">Show Broken Links Only
 </a>
</p>

<?php endif; ?>

<table class="entry-form" >
 <tr>
  <td class="header">Page</td>
  <td class="header">Link</td>
  <td class="header">Status</td>
 </tr>
 <?php foreach ($links as $link): ?>
 <tr>
  <td>
   <a target="_blank" href="<?php echo $link['page']->
     getCollectionPath()?>/">
    <?php echo $link['page']->getCollectionName()?>
   </a>
  </td>
  <td>
   <a target="_blank" href="<?php echo $link['link']?>">
   <?php echo $link['link']?>
   </a>
  </td>
  <td>
   <?php echo $link['status']?>
  </td>
 </tr>
 <?php endforeach; ?>
</table>

</div>
```

What just happened?

The code change we made in the single page for our interface uses the two controller methods illustrated above. We also added a check on the variable `mode` to change the output according to the called controller method.

There are two important things to remember:

1. A call like `$this->set('mode', 'allLinks')` in the controller creates a variable in the single pages called `$mode` with the value `allLinks`. This is the correct way to pass data from the controller to the single page when working with concrete5.

2. When you only specify the controller name in the URL like `http://localhost/index.php/dashboard/reports/broken_links/` the method `view` is called. In case a different method has to be called, it's simply appended to that URL like `http://localhost/index.php/dashboard/reports/broken_links/all/`.

File editor embedded in the dashboard

A topic which has been controversially discussed in the concrete5 community: Some users would like to be able to access and modify all the files on their web space where the concrete5 site is located within the dashboard.

It can be handy to quickly fix an issue with your add-on from your new tablet device while you're on vacation—it could also cause trouble with your partner though. You don't have to remember an FTP account, getting access to the dashboard is enough to do all work on your website, updating content, fixing bugs in the add-ons, and so on.

Certainly, this is something which can be handy, but also a bit dangerous. Changing code on a site which is running on a productive server should be well-thought-out. Being able to make modifications very easily can also break things very quickly. Being able to modify all files within a web application also means that the user account you're using to run the web server must have write access to all the files. By default, concrete5 makes sure that it has access to the directories `files`, `packages`, and `config`; this means that you might not be able to change files in the theme directory unless you change the file permissions.

Building this add-on doesn't harm anyone, but think about it before you actually install it on a productive site of yours. If you use it, it will look like the following:

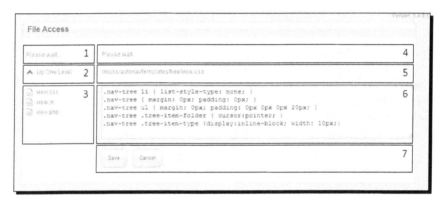

Time for action – creating the file editor add-on

As we're going to create several files for this add-on, we're starting with an overview of the form. It should help you to understand how all the different elements are working together.

The seven boxes shown in the preceding screenshot are the most important elements in the add-on. To make things easier, all elements are visible which is not going to happen once you're working with the add-on. There's no point displaying the **please wait** box if nothing is going on.

Each number is given a name, which is the value we're going to use as the ID of the element:

- 1: `directory-structure-waiting`: only shown when we load new data using our AJAX method to update the directory list.
- 2: `directory-structure-up`: this element is shown if we aren't on the top level to get back to the parent directory.

- ◆ 3: `directory-structure-content`: the actual list of directories and files. Always visible.

- ◆ 4: `file-access-waiting`: the same for the files, displayed when a file is loading and saving.

- ◆ 5: `file-access-caption`: in this element we're going to show the name of the file which is currently open. This is especially helpful, as you can change to another directory while you're still working on the file, which you opened earlier in another directory.

- ◆ 6: `file-access-textarea`: the ID of the textarea where we load the content of the file.

- ◆ 7: `file-access-toolbar`: this element holds all the buttons, which we dynamically show and hide depending on whether a file is loaded or not.

As we're going to create a bunch of files, here's a list with all the files:

- ◆ `packages/c5book/controllers/dashboard/file_access.php`: the second MVC element, our controller which holds everything together.

- ◆ `packages/c5book/single_pages/dashboard/file_access.php`: remember the introduction about MVC? This is the view, which is called single page in concrete5.

- ◆ `packages/c5book/css/file.access.css`: the elements listed above need some styles in order to be arranged properly.

- ◆ `packages/c5book/js/file.access.js`: our add-on uses some AJAX calls; this is where you'll find them.

- ◆ `packages/c5book/helpers/page_permissions.php`: a small helper file to ensure the safety of our AJAX files.

- ◆ `packages/c5book/tools/get_file.php`: the file used by the AJAX script to get the content of a file.

- ◆ `packages/c5book/tools/save_file.php`: another file used by an AJAX method to save a file.

- ◆ `packages/c5book/tools/get_structure.php`: the last file, also used by an AJAX method to get the directory list.

We're going to create each file in the order of the preceding list:

1. Create `packages/c5book/controllers/dashboard/file_access.php` and put the following content in it:

```php
<?php
defined('C5_EXECUTE') or die(_("Access Denied."));

class DashboardFileAccessController extends Controller {
 public $helpers = array('form', 'html');

 public function on_start() {
  $html = Loader::helper('html');

  $this->addHeaderItem($html->css('file.access.css', 'c5book'));
  $this->addHeaderItem($html->javascript('file.access.js',
   'c5book'));
   }

}
?>
```

2. Create the single page `packages/c5book/single_pages/dashboard/file_access.php` with the following content:

```php
<?php
defined('C5_EXECUTE') or die(_("Access Denied."));
?>

<h1><span><?php echo t('File Access')?></span></h1>
<div class="ccm-dashboard-inner" style="min-height:500px;">

 <div id="directory-structure">
  <div id="directory-structure-waiting">Please wait...</div>
  <div id="directory-structure-up">Up One Level</div>
  <div id="directory-structure-content"></div>
 </div>

 <div id="file-access-container">
  <div id="file-access-waiting" style="display:none;">Please
    wait...
  </div>
  <div id="file-access-content" style="display:none;">
   <div id="file-access-caption"></div>
   <textarea id="file-access-textarea"></textarea>
   <div id="file-access-toolbar">
```

```php
<?php
 $ih = Loader::helper('concrete/interface');
 echo $ih->button_js(t('Save'),'fileSave()','left');
 echo $ih->button_js(t('Cancel'),'fileCancel()','left');
 ?>
 </div>
 </div>
 </div>

 <div style="clear:both"></div>

 </div>
```

3. Let's make sure our layout looks as expected and create `packages/c5book/css/file.access.css`:

```css
file-access-folder {
 background:
 url('../../../concrete/images/dashboard/sitemap/folder.png') no-
 repeat;
 padding-left: 22px;
 height: 20px;
 cursor: pointer;
}
file-access-file {
 background:
 url('../../../concrete/images/dashboard/sitemap/document.png')
 no-repeat;
 padding-left: 22px;
 height: 20px;
 cursor: pointer;
}
#directory-structure {
 float:left;
 width:15%;
}
#directory-structure-up {
 background:
 url('../../../concrete/images/dashboard/sitemap/up.png') no-
 repeat;
 padding-left: 22px;
 height: 20px;
 cursor: pointer;
 display: none;
}
#file-access-container {
```

```
  float:left;
  width:85%;
}
#file-access-textarea {
 width:100%;
 min-height:500px;
}
```

4. Next, the file with all the AJAX magic—packages/c5book/js/file.access.js:

```
var currentDirectory = '';
var currentFile = '';

function openDirectory()
{
    $("#directory-structure-waiting").show();
    $("#directory-structure-content").hide();
    $("#directory-structure-up").hide();
    $("#directory-structure-content").html("");

    $.post(CCM_REL + CCM_DISPATCHER_FILENAME +
    '/tools/packages/c5book/get_structure', {directory:
     currentDirectory}, function(data) {

        if (data.folders) {
            $.each(data.folders, function(idx, val) {
                $("#directory-structure-content").append("<div
                    class=\"file-access-folder\">"+val+"</div>");
            })
        }
        if (data.files) {
            $.each(data.files, function(idx, val) {
                $("#directory-structure-content").append("<div
                    class=\"file-access-file\">"+val+"</div>");
            })
        }

        if (currentDirectory != '') {
            $("#directory-structure-up").show();
        }

        $("#directory-structure-waiting").hide();
        $("#directory-structure-content").show();

    }, 'json');
```

```
}

function openFile(filename)
{
   currentFile = currentDirectory + filename;

   $("#file-access-waiting").show();
   $("#file-access-content").hide();

   $.post(CCM_REL + CCM_DISPATCHER_FILENAME +
   '/tools/packages/c5book/get_file',
      {directory: currentDirectory, file: filename},
      function(data) {
         $("#file-access-textarea").val(data.fileContent);
         $("#file-access-caption").text(currentFile);
         $("#file-access-content").show();
         $("#file-access-waiting").hide();
      }, 'json');
}
function fileCancel()
{
   currentFile = '';
   $("#file-access-content").hide();
}
function fileSave()
{
   $("#file-access-waiting").show();
   $("#file-access-content").hide();

   $.post(CCM_REL + CCM_DISPATCHER_FILENAME +
   '/tools/packages/c5book/save_file',
      {file: currentFile, fileContent: $("#file-access-
         textarea").val()},
      function (data) {
         $("#file-access-waiting").hide();
      }, 'json');
}

$(document).ready(function() {
   openDirectory();

   $(".file-access-folder").live("click", function() {
      // append selected directory and reload
      currentDirectory += $(this).text() + "/";
```

```
        openDirectory();
    })

    $(".file-access-file").live("click", function() {
        openFile($(this).text());
    })

    $("#directory-structure-up").click(function() {
        // remove last directory from path and reload
        currentDirectory = currentDirectory.replace(/[\w]*\/$/,"");
        openDirectory();
    });
})
```

5. Next, we have to create our helper which is used in the three PHP files used by AJAX calls. Create `packages/c5book/helpers/page_permissions.php` and put the following content in it:

```php
<?php
class PagePermissionsHelper {
    public static function exitIfNoReadAccess($path) {
        $page = Page::getByPath($path);
        $permissions = new Permissions($page);

        if (!$permissions->canRead()) {
            die();
        }
    }
}
?>
```

6. Our first PHP file `packages/c5book/tools/get_file.php` used by the AJAX methods:

```php
<?php
defined('C5_EXECUTE') or die(_("Access Denied."));
header('Content-type: text/json');

Loader::helper('page_permissions', 'c5book');
PagePermissionsHelper::exitIfNoReadAccess
    ('/dashboard/file_access');

$files = array();
$folders = array();

$directory = './' . $_REQUEST['directory'];
```

```
$file = $_REQUEST['file'];

$ret['fileContent'] = file_get_contents($directory . $file);

echo json_encode($ret);
?>
```

7. The second file for our AJAX methods—packages/c5book/tools/save_file:

```
<?php
defined('C5_EXECUTE') or die(_("Access Denied."));
header('Content-type: text/json');

Loader::helper('page_permissions', 'c5book');
PagePermissionsHelper::exitIfNoReadAccess
    ('/dashboard/file_access');

$file = './' . $_REQUEST['file'];

$ret['returnValue'] = file_put_contents($file,
    $_REQUEST['fileContent']);

echo json_encode($ret);
?>
```

8. Finally, the last AJAX file to load the directory and file structure—packages/c5book/tools/get_structure.php:

```
<?php
defined('C5_EXECUTE') or die(_("Access Denied."));
header('Content-type: text/json');

Loader::helper('page_permissions', 'c5book');
PagePermissionsHelper::exitIfNoReadAccess
    ('/dashboard/file_access');

$ret['items'] = array();

$files = array();
$folders = array();

$directory = './' . $_REQUEST['directory'];
if ($dh = opendir($directory)) {

    while (false !== ($file = readdir($dh))) {
```

```
        if ($file == '.' || $file == '..') continue;

        if (is_dir($directory . $file)) {
            $ret['folders'][] = $file;
        }
        else {
            $ret['files'][] = $file;
        }
    }

    closedir($dh);
}

echo json_encode($ret);
?>
```

What just happened?

If everything worked as planned, you can reinstall the package and a new element `File Access` in your dashboard should appear in the left navigation. If you click on it, the structure should load shortly afterwards and you can navigate around and open text files, edit them, and save the changes. No need to fire up your FTP application for a quick change to the configuration files.

We're going to have a closer look at the controller, as it is a bit uncommon and doesn't completely follow the usual MVC concept.

Controller without logic

If you look at `packages/c5book/controllers/dashboard/file_access.php`, you'll find very few lines of code. Why is there almost no logic in the controller? You remember the introduction—the controller contains all the logic of the add-on. As always in life, it's full of exceptions.

The reason for this is simple: instead of reloading the whole dashboard page with every action, we use AJAX to update only the parts which have actually changed. This not only improves the look and feel, but also the performance.

AJAX always needs a different way to fetch data. This could have been a different method in the controller, but this would usually have been linked to a view. In this case, it's easier to create a completely independent file in the `tools` directory to process the AJAX requests.

What does this mean at the end? The controller is pretty much empty; all the logic has been moved into JavaScript files in combination with some independent `tools`.

The following graphic shows the relationship of all the different elements. As you can see, all the actions go straight to the AJAX scripts and skip the controller, which is only used once when the page is loaded the first time:

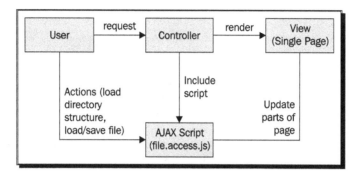

Have a go hero – extending the file editor add-on

This add-on works, but misses quite a few features any end user would expect to find when looking at it. Why not try to add some features?

Here are some ideas:

- Add the ability to download files
- Detect the file type to make sure no one tries to load a binary file like ZIP or JPG into the textarea
- A place to upload a file, maybe with support for auto extracting ZIP files
- Add a breadcrumb navigation to be able to navigate back to a previous directory quicker

Support for different views like a tree structure, thumbnails, and so on. There are plenty of things to do.

Summary

This was the last chapter where you actually built something. In the next and final chapter, we're only going to look at how to deploy your site to a different server as well as a few configurations you can make.

While most customizations and add-ons we created were pretty basic, they should have given you the basic knowledge to build lots of different add-ons. Once you get used to the concrete5 framework, you can build all kinds of add-ons just by knowing what has been discussed so far in combination with some PHP and JavaScript knowledge.

Before you leave this chapter, think about the following things and make sure you know and understand them. These are the basics from this chapter you should know if you build your own dashboard extension:

- A dashboard add-on is basically a single page like any other single page with the exception that it's located underneath the `dashboard` in the sitemap. Please note: these pages are only visible if you tick the checkbox `Show System Pages`.
- You can put several methods in a single controller to process data or change the behavior of the output.
- Look at the graphic at the beginning of this chapter and make sure you understand the separation of each element in the MVC pattern. Something which is also useful to know if you work with other frameworks.

If you need more information about MVC and the process of creating a controller, including methods with parameters, have a look at the following URL:

```
http://www.concrete5.org/documentation/how-tos/developers/basic-mvc-
in-concrete5/
```

11
Deployment and Configuration

In previous chapters we created a number of examples, but not all of them are suited for your website. However, once you clean up everything and add the content you want, you have to make your website available on the Internet.

In the last chapter of this book, you'll find information which might be useful but not necessary during the step by step examples you've seen earlier in this book. The deployment part is also full of hints and not everything you'll see has to apply to your situation; keep that in mind.

Deployment

So far we've done all the work on your local computer, but you'll probably want to publish your website on a web server accessible by the public someday. It's a bit difficult to assume all the possible configurations out there. Every web server is a bit different; there are different operating system, different web server software, and a lot of parameters your hosting company can change.

In this section, you'll find information which should make the process of deploying your website easier, no matter what hosting company you work with. However, keep in mind that it can vary depending on your situation and you might have to adapt to that.

Preparations for deployment

The following steps aren't necessary in every case, but they make the deployment process a bit more solid.

Time for action – disabling pretty URL and cache

Carry out the following steps:

1. In your dashboard, go to **Sitewide Settings** and make sure that the checkbox **Enable Pretty URLs** isn't ticked and then click on **Save** if you had to change it, as shown in the following screenshot:

2. Delete the file named `.htaccess` which is in the root of your site like `index.php`.

3. On the top in the dashboard, locate and select **Debug** to disable the cache.

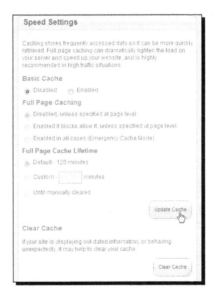

4. First, click on **Clear Cache** to clean up all the files saved in your files directory.

5. Then activate the radio button **Disabled** and then click on **Update Cache**, as shown in the preceding screenshot.

What just happened?

Why did we disable the pretty URLs? concrete5 creates a `.htaccess` file to rewrite the URLs, which is based on a technology by the Apache web server. If you move your website to a server without support for `.htaccess`, your website might be broken after the move.

Please note, without pretty URLs you have to open the login page by using the following address:

`http://localhost/index.php/login`.

The cache does not necessarily break things on your website, but since it's quite difficult to predict what objects you will find in the cache, it is safer to disable it. You can enable it once your website has found its new home. You can find the cached files in this directory `c:/xampplite/htdocs/files/cache`; some can be read quite easily, and some not so much.

Transfer MySQL database

concrete5 uses MySQL to store most of its data found in the pages. It's therefore essential to transfer it to the new server. There are plenty of ways to do this, you might even have some bash scripts to transfer a database from one server to another; if you're that guy, this chapter isn't for you.

We're going to use phpMyAdmin, mostly because it's a widely used tool to manage a MySQL database. The XAMPP stack we've worked with also contains a version of phpMyAdmin, which will make it an easy task to export the database.

Time for action – transferring a MySQL database

Carry out the following steps:

1. If it's not already running, locate the **XAMPP Control Panel** in your start menu and open it. Apache and MySQL should be running, if not start them. Click on **Admin** next to **MySQL** to open phpMyAdmin.

2. In the new phpMyAdmin screen, click on the database named **concrete5**, which you'll find in the left column.

3. A new screen appears where you can activate the **Export** register on the top. Save the data into a plain SQL file including the structure and data. You can see the settings on the next screen:

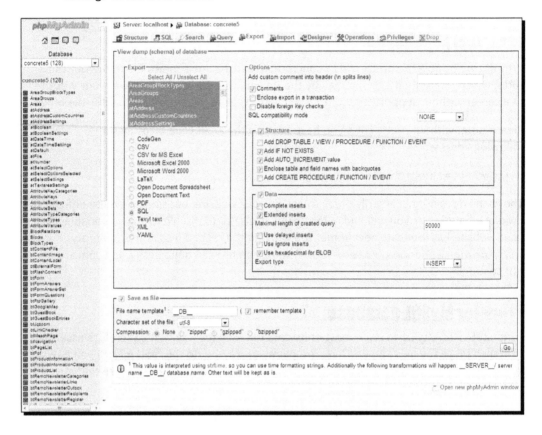

4. After you've clicked on **Go** in the bottom right corner, you'll get a file containing all the data of your database.

5. Now it's time to connect to the new website. Open phpMyAdmin on your new server. If you don't know where to find it, contact your hosting partner.

6. After you've logged in to phpMyAdmin, locate the database on the left, which you want to use for your website. Once you've selected it, click on **Import** on the right screen. Select the file you've just downloaded and click on **Go** at the bottom right corner, as shown in the following screenshot:

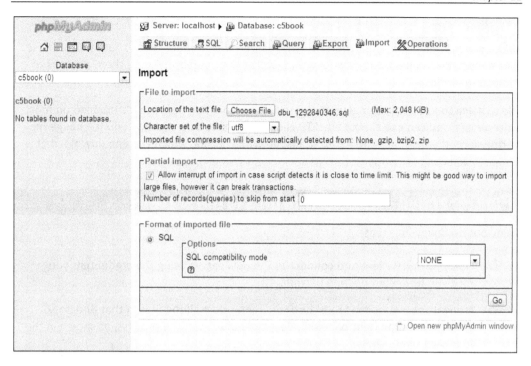

What just happened?

The preceding steps were necessary to transfer the content of our MySQL database to the new server. More experienced users are probably going to skip phpMyAdmin and simply use two commands:

- One to export the database on the Windows computer: `mysqldump -u concrete5 -p concrete5 > sql.dump`

- Another one to import the dump file on the new server: `mysql -u [user-on-new-server] -p [database-on-new-server] < sql.dump`

Not every database is configured the same way. Troubleshooting character sets can be annoying and time consuming; due to the fact that concrete5 uses utf8 all the time, you should try to make sure your database is set up the same way to avoid possible problems.

In the first chapter, we changed the MySQL setting, which made sure that our table names were case sensitive, even on Windows. Without this setting, we would now have lower case table names on a Linux server, which doesn't work, unless someone changed the default setting on the server. If that happened, you'd have to change the server settings or rename every table to its actual name. For example, `areagroupblocktypes` would have to be named `AreaGroupBlockTypes`. In other words, just try to make sure you always work with case sensitive MySQL server configurations to avoid the hassle.

Transferring files to server

When you installed concrete5 you probably realized that it needs quite a lot of files. These files have to be copied to the new server as well as the database. Again, there are tons of options to do this.

We're going to use a traditional unencrypted FTP connection because it's enabled on most web servers. You can use almost any FTP client, just make sure it allows you to change file permissions. If you're not sure about it, just go with FileZilla, which you can download at `http://filezilla-project.org/`.

Time for action – transferring files to the server

Carry out the following steps:

1. Open your FTP client and connect to the new server using the credentials you received from your hosting partner.

2. Navigate to `c:\xampplite\htdocs\` and select all the files in that directory. Drag them to the right pane or select **Upload** to start the process, as shown in the following screenshot:

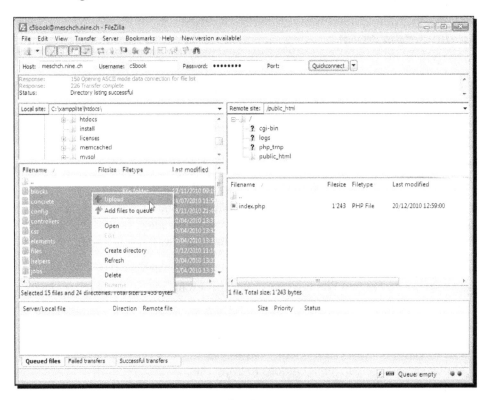

3. Once all the files have been uploaded, it will probably take a while, so you might want to set the file system permissions.

What just happened?

We uploaded all the files from concrete5, as well as our own files added to the website to the new server by using FileZilla.

Due to the fact that concrete5 contains a lot of files, it took a long time to upload all of them. Even a very fast Internet connection won't change a lot. The FTP protocol has some overhead on every file transferred to the server making the process slow as soon as you transfer lots of single files.

If you can extract a ZIP archive or something similar on your server, you should compress all the files into a single file first and upload that and then extract it.

Time for action – updating the configuration file

The URL to access your website changed and so did probably the username and password to access the MySQL database. We have to update the configuration file to match the new values by taking the following steps:

1. Open `config/site.php` and locate each of the following parameters.

2. `DB_SERVER`: this parameter has the value `localhost`, which quite likely will work on your new server as well. Check your hosting information to be sure and modify the value according to your information.

3. `DB_USERNAME`: this parameter has very likely changed; enter the username you want to use to access your MySQL database.

4. `DB_PASSWORD`: another parameter which has probably changed; replace it with the new password to access your MySQL database.

5. `DB_DATABASE`: another parameter you might have to change. Enter the name of the new database where you've imported the MySQL dump in the previous section.

6. `BASE_URL`: concrete5 redirects you to the base URL by default. As the website isn't running on `localhost` any longer, you have to update this value with the website URL that you've received from your hosting partner. You can also disable the base URL redirection by inserting the following line in the PHP block:

```
define('REDIRECT_TO_BASE_URL', false);
```

7. `DIR_REL` doesn't change if you followed this book step by step. It would change if your website had to run in a subdirectory. Enter the path and you're okay.

What just happened?

We modified the configuration file to meet the new values to access your website and MySQL database. Nothing fancy, but it had to be done.

If everything worked as planned, you should now be able to access your website under the new address from your new web server.

Time for action – setting file permissions

This part might be unnecessary, depending on your web server configuration. It's all about making sure that your web server can access the files from your website. The following screenshot shows a simplified graphic without MySQL involved to illustrate the communication between the web server and the files:

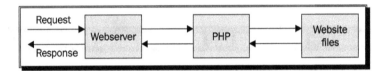

The web server can run under a different user than the PHP and the files can be owned by a different user again. To make things even more difficult, you can use groups instead of users as well. It's pretty hard to predict the configuration of your server; there is therefore no single solution.

If you're running suEXEC or suPHP on Apache, then all the elements run with the same user making your web server more secure, and easier to use in this case. The web server can access and write the files by default; there's no need to change anything.

Accessing (reading) the files shouldn't be a problem. Files written by the FTP server are almost always readable by the web server, but often not writable. The directories `config`, `files`, `packages`, and `updates` should be writable by the web server.

Files on a Linux like server are usually writable by the user but no one else. If you right click on the `files` directory in FileZilla and select **File Permissions**, you'll see a dialog like the one shown in the following screenshot:

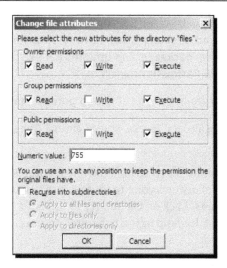

These are the default settings mentioned earlier. The number 755 represents the nine checkboxes in the screenshot. The first number is the owner, the second is the group, and the third is the public.

Each setting has a number which creates the numeric value 755:

- ◆ Execute: 1
- ◆ Write: 2
- ◆ Read: 4

If you add all the selected numbers in the order of owner, group, and public, you'll get 755.

- ◆ Owner: 4 (Read) + 2 (Write) + 1 (Execute) = 7
- ◆ Group: 4 (Read) + 1 (Execute) = 5
- ◆ Public: 4 (Read) + 1 (Execute) = 5

When using FileZilla, you don't really have to care about these numbers, but you'll someday find them very handy when you get into the console.

What do these numbers mean? If your web server doesn't run under the user that owns your files, you won't be able to upload a new file, install a new package, and so on. Here is what you should try to make sure everything works as it should:

1. Try to upload a new file in the file manager. It doesn't matter which method you're using; you can upload a single file or several files by using the advanced multi file uploader. If it works, you're the lucky one who doesn't have to change any settings. If not, continue to step two.

2. We assume that your web server runs under same user that is set as the group owner of your files and directory which have to be writable. Go back to FileZilla and select **config**, **files**, **packages**, and **updates** if it exists. Click on the right mouse button and select **File Permissions** again.

3. Tick the checkbox **Write** in the box of **Group permissions** and click on **Ok**.

4. Try to upload a file again. If it works, you're almost done. If it doesn't work, continue to step five.

5. If your web server cannot even write a file if it's writable by all members of the group, you can only allow everyone to write it and tick the checkbox Write in the box **Public permissions**. Click on **Ok** and try to upload a file again, if it doesn't work, you might have to ask for help in the concrete5 forums.

What just happened?

File permissions can be tricky, especially if you're not used to work with them. Hopefully, the preceding steps worked for you, but due to the vast variety of server configurations, you can never be sure.

There are also some web servers where you can change the file permissions by using an FTP client, even though the dialog is available. In this case, you will probably have to use an interface offered by your hosting company. Get in touch with them or ask for help in the concrete5 community, but post as many details about your problem as you can!

If you're done with the transfer, you might want to enable the cache again. Have a look at the previous paragraph where we changed the cache setting; you can find it in your dashboard under **Sitewide Settings | Debug**.

Configuration

In this chapter, you'll find lots of different options you can set. You will probably have to change them very rarely. Memorizing every part in this chapter isn't going to help you a lot, but try to remember the things you can change in case you've got a project with special requirements.

Updating the configuration file

While there are several options you can change using the concrete5 interface, there are also lots of values you have to set in your configuration files.

In this section you'll find some code snippets. Make sure you paste them between the PHP tags. If the file `config/site.php` looks like the following:

```php
<?php
define('DB_SERVER', 'localhost');
define('DB_USERNAME', 'concrete5');
define('DB_PASSWORD', 'concrete5');
define('DB_DATABASE', 'concrete5');
define('BASE_URL', 'http://www.example.com');
define('DIR_REL', '');
define('PASSWORD_SALT', 'R3nAjizpVw3AbleCFD2e5fZbXzNACYvnxoq');
?>
```

You have to insert the snippets before the closing PHP tag, as follows:

```php
<?php
define('DB_SERVER', 'localhost');
define('DB_USERNAME', 'concrete5');
define('DB_PASSWORD', 'concrete5');
define('DB_DATABASE', 'concrete5');
define('BASE_URL', 'http://www.example.com');
define('DIR_REL', '');
define('PASSWORD_SALT', 'R3nAjizpVw3AbleCFD2e5fZbXzNACYvnxoq');
define('REDIRECT_TO_BASE_URL', 'FALSE');
?>
```

Base URL redirection

On a site where you have more than one URL, you might want to make sure that one address is used as the primary URL. Let's assume we've got two addresses: `http://www.example.com` and `http://www.beispiel.ch`. As your company is located in the United States, you don't want your visitors to stay on `beispiel.ch`. When you look into your generated `site.php` file, you can already find the BASE_URL constant:

```php
define('BASE_URL', 'http://www.example.com');
```

There's another constant which must be set to TRUE:

```php
define('REDIRECT_TO_BASE_URL', 'TRUE');
```

By default, this constant is already set to TRUE, there's no need to change it if you want to use the base URL redirection. If you don't want concrete5 to redirect to the base URL you've entered, simply set REDIRECT_TO_BASE_URL to FALSE.

Multilanguage

You presumably understand English if you're reading this book, but you might still want to use concrete5 in another language.

First, make sure your concrete5 has been translated to the language you're looking for. Check the following project on mygengo to see the current state of the translations:

`http://mygengo.com/string/p/concrete5-1`

If you found your language in an up-to-date state, follow these steps to install the translation.

Time for action – installing a translation file

Carry out the following steps:

1. Open your browser and navigate to `http://mygengo.com/string/p/ concrete5-1.`

2. Look for the language you want to download and get the file and extract it into a local directory.

3. Rename the file matching your concrete5 version to `messages.po`.

4. Go to `http://www.poedit.net/`, download `Poedit`, and install it.

5. Open the `messages.po` file you've downloaded using Poedit.

6. Save the file in Poedit; this will generate a file named `messages.mo` in the same directory as `messages.po`. You should have a `messages.mo` file now. If you've downloaded `de_DE` you have to put `messages.po` in the directory `languages\ de_DE\LC_MESSAGES`. You have to create the subdirectories manually.

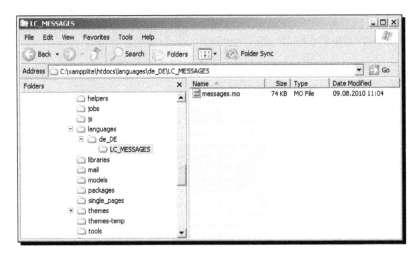

7. Once the files are where they belong, open `config/site.php` in the text editor of your choice.

8. Insert the line `define('LOCALE', 'de_DE');`. It should look like the following:

```php
<?php
define('DB_SERVER', 'localhost');
define('DB_USERNAME', 'concrete5');
define('DB_PASSWORD', 'concrete5');
define('DB_DATABASE', 'concrete5');
define('BASE_URL', 'http://localhost');
define('DIR_REL', '');
define('PASSWORD_SALT',
  'R3nAjizpVw3AbleCFD2e5f2AZkeCuQIzNACYvnxoq');
define('LOCALE', 'de_DE');
?>
```

What just happened?

After you save the file, you can reload concrete5.

You should immediately see the changes in the toolbar at the top, as shown in the following screenshot:

Cache to improve performance

concrete5 uses the Zend Framework for a few things, including caching objects to improve performance. By using the Zend cache concrete5 can save the results of complex queries and procedures to reduce the number of calls, and therefore improve a website's response time. Thanks to Zend, there are lots of options and backends we can use for our cache.

By default, concrete5 uses a simple file cache but there are other backends you can use:

- **SQLite**: Stores the cached objects in a SQLite database.

- **Memcached**: Uses the distribution caching system daemon memcache.

- **APC**: A shared memory caching extension for PHP.

- **XCache**: Another shared memory cache extension.

- **Zend platform**: Used an API from the Zend Platform Product.

- **Zend server**: Zend server offers a disk and a shared memory extension which can be used as well.

- **Static**: Pulls static files to avoid PHP completely. Uses a complex configuration.

The information about the backends has been taken from the following page:

```
http://framework.zend.com/manual/en/zend.cache.html
```

If your web server supports any of the cache extensions, you should try to enable them and make some tests to see if there's any change in the page generation time. Even though XAMPP should be fast enough for your needs, performance can still be an issue. Once you've got lots of hits or lots of concurrent users, things can slow down. If possible, use a cache extension, even if you don't feel any performance issue.

In case you aren't sure about the installed cache extension, create a script with a call to phpinfo.

Time for action – getting PHP information

Carry out the following steps:

1. Create a file named info.php in this directory: c:\xampplite\htdocs.

2. Enter the following lines:
   ```
   <?php
   phpinfo();
   ?>
   ```

3. Open http://localhost/info.php in your web browser.

What just happened?

The PHP information page contains everything about your PHP configuration. In case you haven't seen this page before, make sure you get at least a little bit familiar with it as a lot of people will ask for it when you ask questions in the concrete5 community.

If an extension like APC is enabled, you can find it somewhere in the information page. XAMPP doesn't come with a real cache extension like APC; the only backends we can use are the file system and a SQLite database.

 When you're looking to get support from a community such as concrete5.org, people will often ask you about information you can find in this information page as well. It does reveal lots of information about your configuration, but it helps a lot if you can attach the output of this page to a forum thread if you ask for help.

Activating SQLite

Using SQLite as a cache backend isn't really recommended and not widely used, but as it is an extended backend, it has some additional parameters which make it a nice example, even if you probably don't want to use it on your production server.

♦ First, we have to get all necessary information about our backend from Zend. You'll probably end up being on this page: `http://framework.zend.com/manual/en/zend.cache.backends.html#zend.cache.backends.sqlite`. The page tells us that there's one mandatory parameter we have to set to tell Zend Cache where the cache database should be stored: `cache_db_complete_path`.

♦ Open `config/site.php` and set `CACHE_LIBRARY` and `CACHE_BACKEND_OPTIONS`. The configuration file should look like the following:

```php
<?php
define('DB_SERVER', 'localhost');
define('DB_USERNAME', 'concrete5');
define('DB_PASSWORD', 'concrete5');
define('DB_DATABASE', 'concrete5');
define('BASE_URL', 'http://localhost');
define('DIR_REL', '');
define('PASSWORD_SALT', 'R3nAjizpVw3AbleCFD2e5CkeCuQIzNACYvnxoq');

define('CACHE_LIBRARY', 'Sqlite');
$cacheBackendOptions = array('cache_db_complete_path'=> 'sqlite-
    cache.db');
define('CACHE_BACKEND_OPTIONS', serialize($cacheBackendOptions));
?>
```

Using APC

It doesn't work on XAMPP but if your web host supports it, you should activate APC when you move the website to the production server. It's currently the preferred cache backend of a lot of concrete5 developers and does noticeably improve the performance.

The APC backend doesn't have any options, so you don't have to set
`CACHE_BACKEND_OPTIONS`; only `CACHE_LIBRARY` is needed. The configuration
file should look like the following:

```php
<?php
define('DB_SERVER', 'localhost');
define('DB_USERNAME', 'concrete5');
define('DB_PASSWORD', 'concrete5');
define('DB_DATABASE', 'concrete5');
define('BASE_URL', 'http://localhost');
define('DIR_REL', '');
define('PASSWORD_SALT', 'R3nAjizpVw3AbleCFD2exSwiUzKkbXezNACYvnxoq');

define('CACHE_LIBRARY', 'apc');
?>
```

Measuring the site performance

If you change the cache backend, you probably want to make sure that it actually improves
the performance. It can in fact happen that a cache backend slows down the process instead
of improving it. This might be because of a slow file system, an overloaded database server,
or anything else that runs on your server.

XAMPP installs Apache with a component named **ApacheBench**, a small executable file
named `ab`. This is a simple but nice way to test a website's performance:

1. If you're running Windows, press `Windows+R` and enter `cmd` and confirm it with a
    click on the Ok button.

2. Enter `c:\xampplite\apache\bin\ab.exe -c 5 -n 100 http://localhost/`
    and press *Enter* to confirm the command. The parameter `-c` sets the number of
    concurrent requests to 5 and `-n` sets the number of requests to 100. After a few
    seconds, you should see an output with lots of information—most people care
    about `Requests per second`.

    ```
    H:\>c:\xampplite\apache\bin\ab.exe -c 5 -n 100 http://localhost/
    This is ApacheBench, Version 2.3 <$Revision: 655654 $>
    Copyright 1996 Adam Twiss, Zeus Technology Ltd, http://www.
    zeustech.net/
    Licensed to The Apache Software Foundation, http://www.apache.org/

    Benchmarking localhost (be patient).....done


    Server Software:        Apache/2.2.14
    Server Hostname:        localhost
    ```

```
Server Port:            80

Document Path:          /
Document Length:        8025 bytes

Concurrency Level:      5
Time taken for tests:   27.016 seconds
Complete requests:      100
Failed requests:        0
Write errors:           0
Total transferred:      845700 bytes
HTML transferred:       802500 bytes
Requests per second:    3.70 [#/sec] (mean)
Time per request:       1350.799 [ms] (mean)
Time per request:       270.160 [ms] (mean, across all concurrent
requests)
Transfer rate:          30.57 [Kbytes/sec] received

Connection Times (ms)
             min  mean[+/-sd] median   max
Connect:       0    0   1.6      0      16
Processing:  828 1336 403.5    1313   2922
Waiting:     813 1313 400.2    1281   2891
Total:       828 1336 403.4    1313   2922

Percentage of the requests served within a certain time (ms)
   50%    1313
   66%    1406
   75%    1453
   80%    1484
   90%    1578
   95%    2547
   98%    2891
   99%    2922
  100%    2922 (longest request)
```

Using this simple tool allows you to quickly and easily compare a cache backend. It also offers you a simple way to see if your new web host performs as good as they are saying. Just replace http://localhost/ with the address of your server, but keep in mind that you're going to execute a lot of requests. Don't use this tool for productive servers unless it's your server you're benchmarking.

Summary

You've made it to the end of this book! We hope you enjoyed it and learned how to work with concrete5 to create your own website with some basic customizations. While we recognize that this book does not include the perfect solution for every problem, you now have a few techniques to try out during your investigations.

If anything is unclear, feel free to contact the author at the following website: `http://www.c5book.com`

Pop Quiz Answers

Chapter 1: Installation

Pop Quiz 1

1	a
2	b
3	d
4	Correct answer: a, b, c, and d. However, keep in mind that the core team only supports Apache at the moment. As long as PHP works, you should be able to run concrete5, but if you want to get good support it's recommended to use Apache.

Pop Quiz 2

1	c

Chapter 2: Working with concrete5

Pop Quiz 1

1	Content, HTML, Auto-Nav, External Form, Form, Page List, File, Image, Flash Content, Guestbook, Slideshow, Search, Google Map, Video Player, RSS Displayer, Youtube Video, Survey.
2	<ul><li>Exit Edit Mode to cancel or save the changes you've made to a page</li><li>Properties to change the title of the page, update meta information, and change the values of page attributes</li><li>Design to switch between the theme and page templates</li><li>Versions to look at or approve an older version of the current page</li><li>Move/Delete to remove or move the current page, Dashboard to go back to the dashboard</li><li>Help to get an easy link to answer a question in the community</li><li>Sign Out to exit concrete5</li></ul>
3	<ul><li>Edit Page to activate the edit mode for the current page</li><li>Add Page to add a subpage beneath the current page.</li></ul>

Pop Quiz 2

1	<ul><li>Sitemap to look at a hierarchical structure of your site</li><li>File manager to manage your files available in concrete5</li><li>Reports to check form and survey submissions as well as internal logs</li><li>Users and groups to manage who has access to your site including a register to manage attributes assigned to users to connect more information to each user</li><li>Scrapbook</li><li>Pages and Themes to install and remove themes as well as the ability to add, modify, or remove page types</li><li>Add Functionality, a place to install and remove add-ons available in your site</li><li>System & Maintenance to create and restore database backups</li><li>Sitewide Settings lets you change various options like caching, toolbar of the rich text editor among lots of other things</li></ul>

Chapter 3: Permissions

1	a, c, and e
2	b

Chapter 4: Add-ons

1	a, c, and d

Chapter 5: Creating Your Own Theme

Pop quiz 1

1	a, c, and d

Pop Quiz 2

1	c

Pop Quiz 3

1	b, c, and d

Chapter 6: Creating Your Own Add-on Block

1	a, c, and d

Chapter 9: Everything in a Package

Pop Quiz 1

1	d
2	c

Pop Quiz 2

1	d
2	a and c

Pop Quiz 3

1	d

Index

V

variables
  adding, to handle login errors 122-124
view 243-245
view.php 129, 208
View.php file 90, 91
view method 254

W

web browser 7, 8

X

XAMPP
  about 9, 14
  installing 9, 10
  MySQL settings, modifying 10-12
XAMPP Control Panel Application 13
XCache 282

Z

Zend platform 282
Zend server 282

Thank you for buying
concrete5 Beginner's Guide

About Packt Publishing

Packt, pronounced 'packed', published its first book "*Mastering phpMyAdmin for Effective MySQL Management*" in April 2004 and subsequently continued to specialize in publishing highly focused books on specific technologies and solutions.

Our books and publications share the experiences of your fellow IT professionals in adapting and customizing today's systems, applications, and frameworks. Our solution based books give you the knowledge and power to customize the software and technologies you're using to get the job done. Packt books are more specific and less general than the IT books you have seen in the past. Our unique business model allows us to bring you more focused information, giving you more of what you need to know, and less of what you don't.

Packt is a modern, yet unique publishing company, which focuses on producing quality, cutting-edge books for communities of developers, administrators, and newbies alike. For more information, please visit our website: www.packtpub.com.

About Packt Open Source

In 2010, Packt launched two new brands, Packt Open Source and Packt Enterprise, in order to continue its focus on specialization. This book is part of the Packt Open Source brand, home to books published on software built around Open Source licences, and offering information to anybody from advanced developers to budding web designers. The Open Source brand also runs Packt's Open Source Royalty Scheme, by which Packt gives a royalty to each Open Source project about whose software a book is sold.

Writing for Packt

We welcome all inquiries from people who are interested in authoring. Book proposals should be sent to author@packtpub.com. If your book idea is still at an early stage and you would like to discuss it first before writing a formal book proposal, contact us; one of our commissioning editors will get in touch with you.

We're not just looking for published authors; if you have strong technical skills but no writing experience, our experienced editors can help you develop a writing career, or simply get some additional reward for your expertise.

CMS Design Using PHP and jQuery

ISBN: 978-1-849512-52-7   Paperback: 340 pages

Build and improve your in-house PHP CMS by enhancing it with jQuery

1. Create a completely functional and a professional looking CMS

2. Add a modular architecture to your CMS and create template-driven web designs

3. Use jQuery plugins to enhance the "feel" of your CMS

4. A step-by-step explanatory tutorial to get your hands dirty in building your own CMS

WordPress 3 Complete

ISBN: 978-1-849514-10-1   Paperback: 344 pages

Create your own complete website or blog from scratch with WordPress

1. Learn everything you need for creating your own feature-rich website or blog from scratch

2. Clear and practical explanations of all aspects of WordPress

3. In-depth coverage of installation, themes, plugins, and syndication

4. Explore WordPress as a fully functional content management system

Please check **www.PacktPub.com** for information on our titles

CMS Made Simple 1.6

Create a fully functional and professional website using CMS Made Simple

Beginner's Guide

Sofia Hauschildt

CMS Made Simple 1.6: Beginner's Guide

ISBN: 978-1-847198-20-4   Paperback: 364 pages

Create a fully functional and professional website using CMS Made Simple

1. Learn everything there is to know about setting up a professional website in CMS Made Simple

2. Implement your own design into CMS Made Simple with the help of the easy-to-use template engine

3. Create photo galleries with LightBox and implement many other JQuery effects like interactive navigation in your website

4. Build an eStore and grasp the intricacies of setting up an integrated PayPal checkout

PHP 5 CMS
Framework Development
Second Edition

Expert insight and practical guidance to create an efficient, flexible, and robust web-oriented PHP 5 framework

Martin Brampton

PHP 5 CMS Framework Development - 2nd Edition

ISBN: 978-1-849511-34-6   Paperback: 416 pages

Expert insight and practical guidance to create an efficient, flexible, and robust web-oriented PHP 5 framework

1. Learn about the design choices involved in the creation of advanced web oriented PHP systems

2. Build an infrastructure for web applications that provides high functionality while avoiding pre-empting styling choices

3. Implement solid mechanisms for common features such as menus, presentation services, user management, and more

Please check **www.PacktPub.com** for information on our titles

www.ingramcontent.com/pod-product-compliance
Lightning Source LLC
Chambersburg PA
CBHW080353060326
40689CB00019B/3992